Grade 6

Treasures

Grammar

AND

Writing

Handbook

Macmillan/McGraw-Hill

A

The *McGraw·Hill* Companies

 **Macmillan McGraw-Hill**

Published by Macmillan/McGraw-Hill, of McGraw-Hill Education, a division of The McGraw-Hill Companies, Inc.,
Two Penn Plaza, New York, New York 10121.

Printed in the United States of America

1 2 3 4 5 6 7 8 9 079 11 10 09 08 07

Writing

Contents

4

Writing

Grammar

Contents

Build Skills

Troubleshooter

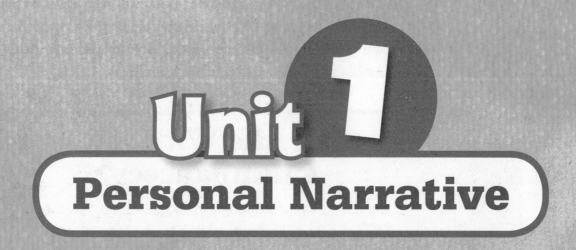

Unit 1
Personal Narrative

Personal Narrative

Significant events happen in everyone's life. A story that tells an individual's experience is called a personal narrative. A personal narrative is a way of sharing a particularly memorable event or of telling about important feelings. It tells the reader how the writer felt about an experience.

Learning from Writers

Read the following examples of personal narrative. What stories do the writers tell? Why do you think they wanted to share their experiences? As you read, look for phrases from each example that show the author's feelings.

THINK AND WRITE

Purpose
Why are personal narratives such an effective form of writing? Write a brief explanation.

My Life With the Chimpanzees

Once, as I walked through thick forest in a downpour, I suddenly saw a chimp hunched in front of me. Quickly I stopped. Then I heard a sound from above. I looked up and there was a big chimp there, too. When he saw me he gave a loud, clear wailing wraaaah—a spine-chilling call that is used to threaten a dangerous animal. To my right I saw a large black hand shaking a branch and bright eyes glaring threateningly through the foliage. Then came another savage wraaaah from behind. Up above, the big male began to sway the vegetation. I was surrounded. I crouched down, trying to appear as nonthreatening as possible.

Suddenly a chimp charged straight toward me. His hair bristled with rage. At the last minute he swerved and ran off. I stayed still. Two more chimps charged nearby. Then, suddenly, I realized I was alone again. All the chimps had gone.

Only then did I realize how frightened I had been. When I stood up my legs were trembling!

—Jane Goodall, from *My Life With the Chimpanzees*

My First Baseball Game

I used to watch baseball on television when I was little, but that's not the same as watching it live. Then one day my dad told me that we were going to the Detroit Tigers game. I went wild!

When we got there, the stadium was already crowded. The fantastic smell of hot dogs lingered in the air. We walked through tunnels to get to left field. Bright lights helped me see the players doing their warm-ups.

Soon, the intercom blared with the names of the players for Detroit and for Milwaukee. When all the players had been named, the umpire walked to home plate, took a brush from his back pocket, and dusted the plate until it was gleaming white. Then he yelled at the top of his lungs, "Play ball!"

—Eric Rice

PRACTICE AND APPLY

Thinking Like a Reader

1. What descriptive words and phrases did Jane Goodall use to explain why the chimps were frightening in "My Life With the Chimpanzees"?

2. What descriptions that appeal to the senses did the author of "My First Baseball Game" use?

Thinking Like a Writer

3. What time-order words signal the order of events in "My Life With the Chimpanzees"?

4. How does the author of "My First Baseball Game" express his joy when his dad asks him to the game?

5. **Reading Across Texts** Reread the two literature models. Compare their beginning, middle, and end.

Features of a Personal Narrative

DEFINITIONS AND FEATURES

A personal narrative tells about something that happened to you and how you felt about it. A good personal narrative:

▶ Expresses the writer's feelings about a **personal experience**.

▶ Uses the **first-person point of view**.

▶ Has an interesting **beginning, middle,** and **end**.

▶ Places events in a **logical sequence**.

▶ Uses **time-order words** to show the sequence of events and to make transitions from one idea to the next.

▶ A Personal Experience

Reread "My Life With the Chimpanzees" by Jane Goodall on page 8. How did the author feel when she encountered the chimps?

> Only then did I realize how frightened I had been. When I stood up my legs were trembling!

The author expresses the terror she felt in her encounter.

▶ First-Person Point of View

In her narrative, Jane Goodall uses the first-person point of view. This means she narrates her own experiences, using the words *I*, *me*, and *my*. How does reading her own words make you feel about her story?

> To my right I saw a large black hand shaking a branch and bright eyes glaring threateningly through the foliage.

The first-person point of view allows you to read the author's own words as she relates her experiences and shows you her feelings about the event.

▶ A Beginning, Middle, and End

A strong narrative needs to include an interesting beginning, middle, and end to seize and hold the reader's attention. Reread the following sentence from the first paragraph.

> Once, as I walked through thick forest in a downpour, I suddenly saw a chimp hunched in front of me.

Notice how the author uses a direct and straightforward approach to begin her narrative.

▶ A Logical Sequence of Events

Jane Goodall describes her encounter with the chimps in a logical sequence. Notice how the sentences inform the reader that Goodall's predicament is becoming more frightening.

> Then I heard a sound from above. I looked up and there was a big chimp there, too.

How did the author set up the action to follow?

▶ Time-Order Words

To help the reader clearly understand the events from beginning to end, time-order words and phrases should be used. Time-order words and phrases include *first, next, finally, the following day, at the last minute,* and *last year.*

> At the last minute he swerved and ran off.

What time-order phrase did the author use?

PRACTICE AND APPLY

Create a Features Chart

1. List the features of a good personal narrative.
2. Reread "My First Baseball Game" by Eric Rice on page 9.
3. Write one example of each feature in Eric's writing.
4. Write what you liked about Eric's personal narrative.

Features	Examples

Prewrite

A personal narrative is a story that describes your own experiences. Writing a personal narrative allows you the chance to share meaningful events from your life.

Purpose and Audience

The purpose of writing a personal narrative is to communicate your thoughts and feelings about a particular experience. It is also to interest or entertain your audience—the reader.

Before writing, think about your audience. Who is going to be reading your personal narrative? How will you communicate your ideas to your audience? Remember always to use the first person, the "I" voice, when writing a personal narrative.

Choose a Topic

Begin by **brainstorming** a list of memorable events from your life. Think about which event would be most interesting to your readers. Also, think about which event you remember the most vividly.

After choosing a topic, **explore ideas** by making a list of details you remember about the experience. Remember to include your own feelings and thoughts. Later, you will organize these ideas.

THINK AND WRITE

Audience

How will your audience affect the way you plan and write your personal narrative? Write your response in your journal.

I explored these ideas by remembering my experiences.

We went to Yellowstone Park

Visited grandparents with brothers

Hour to set up tents

Hiked trails

Climbed mountains

Many different kinds of animals

Saw lots of plants

Then I saw the bear fishing

I took the bear's picture!

Organize • Sequence

In a personal narrative, events happen in a certain order, or sequence. You can plan your narrative by organizing your ideas into a sequence-of-events chart. Some events may not be necessary to tell your story. What changes did the writer make to his original list?

PREWRITE

DRAFT

REVISE

PROOFREAD

PUBLISH

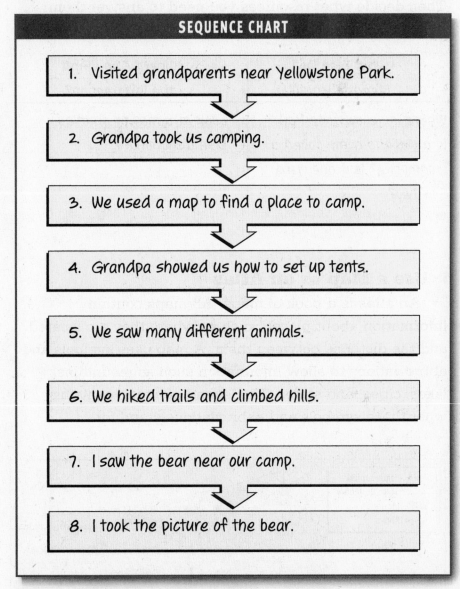

SEQUENCE CHART

1. Visited grandparents near Yellowstone Park.

2. Grandpa took us camping.

3. We used a map to find a place to camp.

4. Grandpa showed us how to set up tents.

5. We saw many different animals.

6. We hiked trails and climbed hills.

7. I saw the bear near our camp.

8. I took the picture of the bear.

PRACTICE AND APPLY

Plan Your Own Personal Narrative

1. Think about your purpose and audience.

2. Brainstorm events and experiences.

3. Select a topic that would make an interesting story.

4. Explore different ideas, thoughts, and feelings.

5. Organize your ideas.

Checklist ✔

Prewriting

- Have you considered your audience and your purpose?

- Have you brainstormed a list of events and experiences?

- Have you selected a topic and explored ideas?

- Have you carefully organized your ideas on a sequence chart?

- Do you need to do any research?

13

Prewrite • Research and Inquiry

Writing PROCESS

▶ Writer's Resources

To get more information for your personal narrative, you may have to do research. Develop a list of questions. Then decide what resources you need to answer them.

What Else Do I Need to Know?	Where Can I Find the Information?
Where is Yellowstone Park? Is a place to camp called a campsite? Is it one word or two?	Look at a map or an atlas. Use a dictionary.

▶ Use a Map or an Atlas

An atlas is a book of maps. All maps contain information about places, such as where they are located and the distance between them. A map uses symbols and abbreviations to show information such as mountains, lakes, cities, and states. The legend of a map explains what these symbols and abbreviations stand for.

The legend explains what each symbol on a map stands for.

The compass rose indicates the directions on the map.

The scale tells how much smaller maps are than the actual places they show.

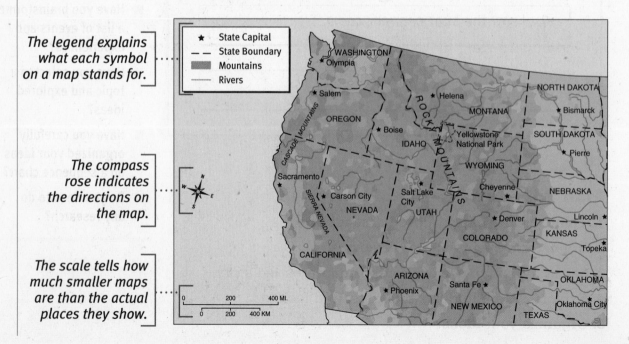

► Look Up Words in a Dictionary

If you are not sure of the meaning or spelling of a word, look it up in a dictionary. Remember that dictionary entries are arranged alphabetically and that several meanings may be listed next to each entry.

► Use Your Research

Use the new information from your research to sharpen the focus of your sequence-of-events chart. This writer added information from a map and checked a word in the dictionary. What additions did he make to his chart?

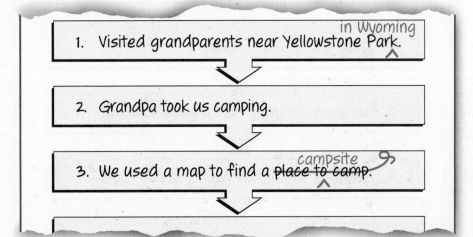

1. Visited grandparents near Yellowstone Park. *in Wyoming*

2. Grandpa took us camping.

3. We used a map to find a ~~place to camp~~. *campsite*

PRACTICE AND APPLY

Review Your Plan

1. Review your sequence-of-events chart.

2. List any questions you have about the topic.

3. Identify the resources you need to answer your questions.

4. Add new information to your chart.

Checklist ✔

Research and Inquiry

- Did you create a list of questions?

- Did you identify possible resources?

- Did you take clear notes?

Draft • Main Idea and Details

Before you start writing your personal narrative, review your chart. Look for main ideas on your chart and make a new paragraph for each main idea. Support the main ideas with details.

Writing PROCESS

SEQUENCE CHART

1. Visited grandparents near Yellowstone Park. *in Wyoming*

2. Grandpa took us camping.

3. We used a map to find a place to camp. *campsite*

4. Grandpa showed us how to set up tents.

5. We saw many different animals.

6. We hiked trails and climbed hills.

7. I saw the bear near our camp.

8. I took the picture of the bear.

Main idea for second paragraph: We went camping.

Supporting details: We found a campsite, set up a tent, hiked, saw many animals.

This is the main idea of my personal narrative. I should mention it in my first paragraph.

✔ Checklist

Drafting

- Does your narrative fit your purpose and audience?

- Does it have an interesting beginning, middle, and end?

- Have you arranged your draft into paragraphs?

- Have you included your thoughts and feelings?

- Have you used vivid words?

Look at how this writer used his chart to write a draft of the narrative. He added details about his experience and shared his feelings about it.

DRAFT

My brothers and I visited my grandparents they live near Yellowstone National Park in Wyoming. I'll never forget the day I photografed a bear.

Main idea of personal narrative

Soon after we arrived Grandpa decided to take us camping in the park. We used a map to find a

Main idea of second paragraph

campsite. It was by a beuatiful pond where there were tall mountains. Grandpa showed us how to set up tents. We hiked trails and climbed hills. We encountered many different kinds of animals but the biggest was the bear. I saw the bear across the pond near our campsite.

Supporting details follow a sequence.

It was busy catching fish. I aimed the camera at it. I moved to get a good shot. It looked at me. I panicked. I clicked the camera anyway. I still have that picture of the bear.

Main idea is restated in final paragraph.

PRACTICE AND APPLY

Draft Your Own Personal Narrative

1. Review your prewriting chart.
2. Organize supporting details around the main ideas.
3. Use time-order words to show a sequence of events.
4. Express feelings in your own voice.
5. Be sure you have a clear beginning, middle, and end.

TECHNOLOGY

Review your draft for logical order. Do the ideas flow smoothly? If not, try moving paragraphs or sentences around by cutting and pasting text.

Revise

Writing PROCESS

Elaborate

One way to improve your writing is to elaborate. When you elaborate, you add important ideas and details that might be missing from your writing. When you revise your personal narrative, you may need to tell more about your feelings.

The writer added details to describe how he feels.

> the best   We found one
> We used a map to find a campsite. ~~It was~~ by a
>   stood like tall soldiers
> beuatiful pond where ~~there were tall~~ mountains.
> They made us feel safe.

The writer uses a descriptive detail to add more excitement in his writing.

> We encountered many different kinds of animals but
> and the meanest of all
> the biggest was the bear.

Word Choice

Choosing the right words for your topic and audience is important when you are writing.

In a personal narrative, select words that will help you sequence the events of your story in a logical order.

> Then,   Later,
> Grandpa showed us how to set up tents. We hiked
>
> trails and climbed hills.

TIME-ORDER WORDS

first

next

then

last

finally

yesterday

tomorrow

after

before

one day

later

as soon as

Better Sentences

As you continue to revise your draft, check your sentences to make sure they fit together. Read the sentences aloud. How do they sound? Do they flow well? Have you included different types of sentences? Have you used sentences of different lengths?

Sometimes you can combine two short sentences into one compound or complex sentence that is more interesting. You may also want to add more information to a short sentence.

> Since I didn't think it was looking
> It was busy catching fish. I aimed the camera at
> When
> it. I moved to get a good shot. It looked at me. I
> or but
> panicked. I clicked the camera anyway.

PRACTICE AND APPLY

Revise Your Own Personal Narrative

1. Use time-order words to show the sequence of events.

2. Elaborate on ideas to create a full picture for the reader.

3. Use language that expresses your feelings distinctly.

4. Grammar Did you use different types of sentences in your writing?

TECHNOLOGY

Find out how to adjust line spacing on the computer. Double space your draft so that you will have more room to mark edits and corrections.

Revise • Peer Conferencing

Now is a good time to take a break from writing. Give a copy of your draft to a partner to read. Read your partner's writing, too. You may be able to give each other ideas on how to improve your narratives.

Writing PROCESS

> Your voice is very clear. I can tell that this really happened to you.

> This main idea could be a good beginning.

> Add time-order words to show sequence of events.

> Add details to create more excitement.

My brothers and I visited my grandparents they live near Yellowstone National Park in Wyoming. I'll never forget the day I photografed a bear.

Soon after we arrived Grandpa decided to take us camping in the park. We used a map to find a campsite. It was by a beuatiful pond where there were tall mountains. Grandpa showed us how to set up tents. We hiked trails and climbed hills. We encountered many different kinds of animals but the biggest was the bear. I saw the bear across the pond near our campsite.

It was busy catching fish. I aimed the camera at it. I moved to get a good shot. It looked at me. I panicked. I clicked the camera anyway. I still have that picture of the bear.

Conferencing for the Reader

■ Are these features of a personal narrative included?
- personal experience
- first-person point of view
- interesting beginning, middle, and end
- events in sequence that makes sense
- time-order words

■ Make sure to tell your partner what is good about the piece, as well as what needs improvement.

As you continue to revise your writing, think about your writing partner's suggestions. This writer made some changes based on his partner's suggestions.

REVISE

were visiting

My brothers and I visited my grandparents they

live near Yellowstone National Park in Wyoming. I'll

never forget the day I photografed a bear.

Soon after we arrived Grandpa decided to take us

First,   the best

camping in the park. We used a map to find a

We found one

campsite. It was by a beuatiful pond where there were

stood like tall soldiers. They made us feel safe. Then,

tall mountains. Grandpa showed us how to set up tents.

Later, winding   steep

We hiked trails and climbed hills. We encountered many

and meanest of all

different kinds of animals but the biggest was the bear.

The next day,

I saw the bear across the pond near our campsite.

Since I didn't think it was looking

It was busy catching fish. I aimed the camera at

When   and growled

it. I moved to get a good shot. It looked at me. I

but

panicked. I clicked the camera anyway. I still have

lifelike

that picture of the bear.

Checklist ✓

Revising

- **Does your story fit your audience and purpose?**

- **Do you need to elaborate on any part of your story?**

- **Did you convey your feelings through colorful language?**

- **Did you use time-order words?**

- **Do your sentences flow smoothly when read aloud?**

PRACTICE AND APPLY

Revise Your Own Personal Narrative

1. Read your draft aloud. Do the words flow smoothly?

2. Use elaboration to explain ideas that might be unclear.

3. Note down your partner's comments, and use these to revise your draft.

Writing PROCESS

Proofread/Edit

After you have revised your narrative, you will need to proofread and edit it to locate and correct any errors in mechanics, grammar and usage, and spelling.

STRATEGIES FOR PROOFREADING

- **Reread your story several times.** If you look for a different type of error each time, you will have a better chance of finding all mistakes.

- **Read each sentence.** Check capitalization and punctuation.

- **Check for spelling mistakes.** Read your narrative from the last word to the first word to focus on spelling.

- **Check for run-on sentences.** Correct them by making two sentences or forming a compound or complex sentence.

TiP!

Spelling

The sound /f/ at the end of a word may be spelled *f, ff, ph,* or *gh.*

REVIEW THE RULES

GRAMMAR

- A compound sentence is made up of two complete sentences joined by a comma and the conjunction *and*, *but*, or *or*.

- A complex sentence contains an independent clause and one or more dependent clauses.

MECHANICS

- Capitalize the first word of a sentence and use the correct end punctuation.

- Use a comma before the conjunction in a compound sentence or after an introductory dependent clause.

- Use a semicolon to separate two parts of a compound sentence not joined by a conjunction.

- A run-on sentence incorrectly joins together two or more sentences that should be written separately or rewritten as a compound or complex sentence.

Go to pages 138–173 to review other rules.

Look at the proofreading corrections made on the draft below. What does the symbol ⌗ mean? Why did the writer begin a new paragraph?

PROOFREAD

~~were visiting~~
My brothers and I ~~visited~~ my grandparents they live near Yellowstone National Park in Wyoming. I'll never forget the day I ~~photografed~~ a bear.

Soon after we arrived, Grandpa decided to take us camping in the park. We used a map to find *the best* campsite. It was by a ~~beuatiful~~ pond where ~~there were~~ *stood like tall soldiers.* They made us feel safe. Then, tall mountains. Grandpa showed us how to set up tents. *Later,* We hiked *winding* trails and climbed *steep* hills. We encountered many different kinds of animals, but the biggest *and meanest of all* was the bear. ⌗ *The next day,* I saw the bear across the pond near our campsite. no ⌗ It was busy catching fish. *Since I didn't think it was looking,* I aimed the camera at it. *When* I moved to get a good shot, It looked at me *and growled.* I panicked, *but* I clicked the camera anyway. I still have *lifelike* that picture of the bear.

First, *We found one* campsite.

Checklist ✓
Proofreading

- Did you check the spelling of new or difficult words in a dictionary?

- Did you use commas and semicolons correctly?

- Did you check for correct sentence capitalization and punctuation?

- Did you correct run-on sentences?

PROOFREADING MARKS

⌗	new paragraph
∧	add
℘	take out
≡	Make a capital letter.
/	Make a small letter.
ⓢⓟ	Check the spelling.
⊙	Add a period.

PRACTICE AND APPLY

Proofread Your Own Personal Narrative

1. Check for misspelled words.

2. Check for correct end punctuation and capitalization.

3. Correct run-on sentences.

4. Use commas in compound sentences and before introductory dependent clauses.

Publish

The final step before publishing your piece is to review it one last time. Using a checklist can help you stay organized.

✓ Self-Check Personal Narrative

❑ **What was my purpose? Did I describe a personal experience?**

❑ **Did I use my own voice to tell my story?**

❑ **Does my narrative have an interesting beginning, middle, and end?**

❑ **Did I use descriptive language to express my feelings?**

❑ **Did I use time-order words to show a sequence of events that makes sense?**

❑ **Do my sentences flow well? Did I use a variety of sentence types?**

❑ **Did I correctly use compound and complex sentences?**

❑ **Did I proofread carefully and correct all errors?**

The writer used the checklist to review his narrative. Read "The Day I Photographed a Bear" and discuss it in a small group. Was it ready to be published? Why or why not?

The Day I Photographed a Bear
by Hector Sanchez

I'll never forget the day I photographed a bear. My brothers and I were visiting my grandparents. They live near Yellowstone National Park in Wyoming.

Soon after we arrived, Grandpa decided to take us camping in the park. First, we used a map to find the best campsite. We found one by a beautiful pond where mountains stood like tall soldiers. They made us feel safe. Then, Grandpa showed us how to set up tents. Later, we hiked winding trails and climbed steep hills. We encountered many different kinds of animals, but the biggest and meanest of all was the bear.

The next day, I saw the bear across the pond near our campsite. It was busy catching fish. Since I didn't think it was looking, I aimed the camera at it. When I moved to get a good shot, it looked at me and growled. I panicked, but I clicked the camera anyway. I still have that lifelike picture of the bear.

TECHNOLOGY

Does your school have a Web site? If possible, use your school's technological resources to publish your narrative on the Internet.

PRACTICE AND APPLY

Publish Your Own Personal Narrative

1. Check your revised draft one more time.

2. Make a neat final copy of your narrative.

3. Submit your narrative to a class or school newspaper.

Personal Narrative

Score	Description
4 Excellent	■ provides an entertaining account about a personal experience and includes thoughts and feelings ■ presents details in an easy-to-follow sequence ■ always uses the first person and clearly expresses feelings ■ uses many time-order words ■ uses complete sentences of varied types and lengths ■ is free or almost free of errors
3 Good	■ tells about a personal experience and includes some thoughts and feelings ■ presents details in the correct order ■ mostly uses the first person and expresses feelings ■ uses some time-order words ■ includes both simple and compound sentences ■ has minor errors that do not confuse the reader
2 Fair	■ tells about a personal experience but focus often strays ■ tells some events out of order ■ does not always use the first person and does not express enough feelings ■ lacks time-order words ■ uses only simple sentences that sometimes require rereading ■ makes frequent errors that confuse the reader
1 Unsatisfactory	■ does not share a personal experience and is not focused or entertaining ■ tells events out of order and is confusing ■ does not use first person and does not express feelings or personality ■ does not use time-order words ■ sentences are choppy, fragments, or run together ■ makes serious and repeated errors

Go to www.macmillanmh.com for a 6-Point Student Writing Rubric.

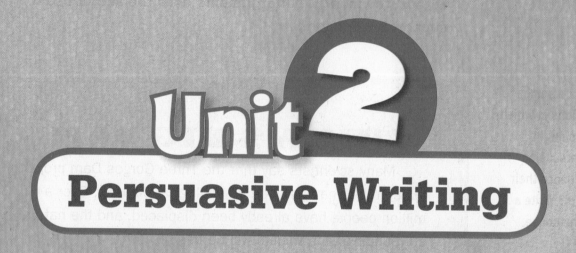

Unit 2
Persuasive Writing

Persuasive Writing

Have you ever tried to convince someone that your opinion was correct? You were using persuasion. In persuasive writing, an author uses logical arguments to convince the reader to support an opinion.

Learning from Writers

Read the following example of persuasion. What is the author's opinion? What arguments does the author use to support his opinion?

THINK AND WRITE

Purpose

What are some situations in which writers might use persuasion to influence their readers? Write a brief response.

CHINA'S BIG DAM

Many scientists say that the Three Gorges Dam project in central China has been an ecological disaster. Over a million people have already been displaced, and the natural surroundings and wildlife will be destroyed.

By blocking the flow of the Yangtze River, the dam created a 370-mile-long lake, or reservoir, west of the city of Yichang. The rising water has swallowed hundreds of deserted towns and villages.

The reservoir will also threaten the habitats of hundreds of fish, plant, and animal species. Among the creatures most at risk: rare river dolphins, clouded leopards, and Siberian white cranes. The government promises to monitor the environment around the dam and has set aside money to create a protective area for the dolphins.

But scientists warn that blocking the river will create sewage backups and may even cause more floods. Some fear that the dam may collapse.

— Adapted from an article in *Time for Kids*

A Wrinkle in Time by Madeleine L'Engle

An evil force, a brain, blocks out stars and imprisons any scientists who try to investigate. Charles Wallace and Meg are the intrepid young people who must challenge the heartless brain in order to rescue their captive father.

If this sounds exciting to you, then you will certainly enjoy reading A Wrinkle in Time by Madeleine L'Engle. It's much more than a fantasy of intergalactic travel and imaginary future worlds. The characters in A Wrinkle in Time face some fantastic problems, but they are also ordinary, recognizable people with problems familiar to any reader.

The exotic setting, constantly surprising events, and interesting and sympathetic characters all contribute to the success of this beautifully written, unforgettable novel.

–Noah Rollins

PRACTICE AND APPLY

Thinking Like a Reader

1. What opinion does the author of "China's Big Dam" express?

2. What arguments does the author of the book report on *A Wrinkle in Time* offer to back up his opinion about the book?

Thinking Like a Writer

3. Why do you think the author wants to convince the reader that his opinion is right?

4. Which of his arguments do you think the author of the book review considers the strongest? Why?

5. **Reading Across Texts** Notice the ways in which the literature models use logical arguments to support their opinions. Write about how the approaches used are alike and different.

Features of Persuasive Writing

DEFINITIONS AND FEATURES

Persuasive writing states the opinion of the writer and attempts to influence the audience. Writing that persuades:

▶ Clearly **states an opinion** on a specific topic.

▶ Supports the opinion with **convincing reasons and arguments**.

▶ Presents reasons in a **logical order**.

▶ Often saves the **strongest argument for last**.

▶ Uses **opinion words**.

▶ States an Opinion

Reread "China's Big Dam" from *Time for Kids* on page 28. What is the author's opinion?

> Many scientists say that the Three Gorges Dam project in central China has been an ecological disaster. Over a million people have already been displaced, and the natural surroundings and wildlife will be destroyed.

The "ecological disaster" referred to is an opinion. Both people and nature, the author believes, will be affected.

▶ Convincing Reasons and Arguments

What reasons does the author present to convince readers that the dam represents an ecological disaster?

> The reservoir will also threaten the habitats of hundreds of fish, plant, and animal species. Among the creatures most at risk: rare river dolphins, clouded leopards, and Siberian white cranes.

How do you think these arguments influence the reader?

▶ Logical Order

The author presents his reasons and arguments in a logical order, one that will make sense to the reader.

> The rising water has swallowed hundreds of deserted towns and villages. The reservoir will also threaten the habitats of hundreds of fish, plant, and animal species.

Which argument does the author present first? Why do you think he chose to use it first?

▶ Save the Strongest Argument for Last

The author saves his strongest argument for last because the last reason given is the one most likely to be remembered.

> But scientists warn that blocking the river will create sewage backups and may even cause more floods. Some fear that the dam may collapse.

By saving his strongest argument for last, the author takes full advantage of his final chance to influence the reader.

▶ Opinion Words

Writers of persuasive pieces should include opinion words in order to make their feelings clear.

> . . . may even cause more floods . . . Some fear . . .

Using opinion words helps make the writer's argument clear. These words also help evoke emotion from the reader.

PRACTICE AND APPLY

Create a Features Chart

1. Reread the book review of *A Wrinkle in Time*.
2. In the Features column, list the features of persuasive writing.
3. In the Examples column, write an example of how the author applied the feature.

Features	Examples

Prewrite

Persuasive writing presents the opinions of the writer and attempts to influence the opinion of the reader. Writing a persuasive piece allows you to share your opinions with others and convince them to agree with you.

Purpose and Audience

The purpose of persuasive writing is to convince your reader that your opinion is correct. Your opinion must be presented logically and with details so that the reasons for your position are clear. Choose words carefully as they can also have an effect on the reader. Before writing, think about your audience. Where will the piece appear? Who will read it?

Choose a Topic

Imagine that you are going to write a letter to the editor of a newspaper. Begin by **brainstorming** a list of topics on which you have strong opinions. Which topic would you like to share with your audience?

Now that you have chosen a topic, **explore ideas** by making a list of your reasons why you had such a strong opinion about it. Later, you will organize your list of ideas.

THINK AND WRITE

Audience
Write what kinds of reasons and arguments will most strongly influence your audience.

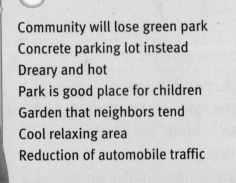

My writing group and I explored these ideas.

Community will lose green park
Concrete parking lot instead
Dreary and hot
Park is good place for children
Garden that neighbors tend
Cool relaxing area
Reduction of automobile traffic

Organize • Problem and Solution

How you organize your reasons to support an opinion can determine how effectively you can convince your audience. Plan your letter to the editor by using a problem and solution organizer. Not all ideas may fit in. Which ideas in her list did the writer leave out?

PREWRITE

DRAFT

REVISE

PROOFREAD

PUBLISH

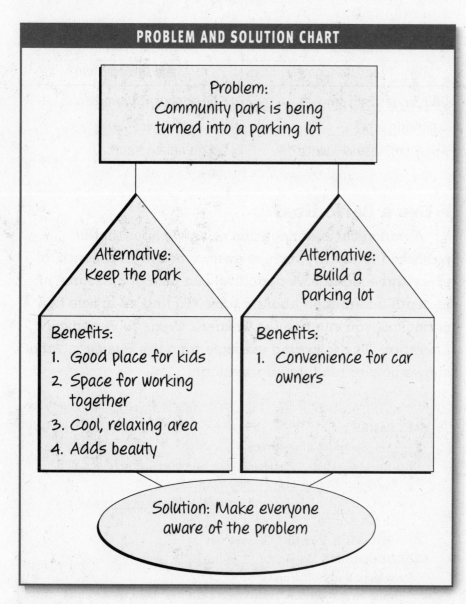

PROBLEM AND SOLUTION CHART

Problem:
Community park is being turned into a parking lot

Alternative: Keep the park

Alternative: Build a parking lot

Benefits:
1. Good place for kids
2. Space for working together
3. Cool, relaxing area
4. Adds beauty

Benefits:
1. Convenience for car owners

Solution: Make everyone aware of the problem

Checklist ✓
Prewriting

- Have you thought about your purpose and audience?

- Have you chosen a topic about which you have a strong opinion?

- Have you explored convincing reasons and arguments about your topic?

- Did you organize your ideas on the problem and solution map?

- Have you thought about opinion words to influence your reader?

- Do you need to do any research?

PRACTICE AND APPLY

Plan Your Own Persuasive Writing

1. Think about your purpose and audience.

2. Brainstorm ideas for a topic that is important to you.

3. Choose a problem and explore possible solutions.

4. Organize your ideas and think of detailed examples.

Writing PROCESS

Prewrite • Research and Inquiry

▶ Writer's Resources

You may have to do research to get more information for your persuasive writing. First, make a list of questions. Then decide what resources you need to answer your questions.

What Else Do I Need to Know?	Where Can I Find the Information?
Who benefits from parking lots?	Check recent periodicals.
To whom should I write?	Do an online search.

▶ Use a Periodical

A periodical is a magazine or newspaper that is published regularly, such as every week, every month, or every three months. A periodical can be a good source of in-depth information about a topic. To find an article in a periodical, you can use the *Reader's Guide to Periodical Literature*. The following example from the *Reader's Guide* shows how to read its information.

Subject heading ···· CITY PARKS

Article title ····   *See also* Village Greens

        Patches of Green in Concrete Jungles [work of Alegria Imperial] il

Issue date ····   *The Green Thumb* 111: 17–22 Mr/Ap '01

Magazine title ···· Pond in a City Park, a Natural Habitat. V. Rivers. *Nature and You*

        24: 6–9 Sep '99

Cross-reference ···· CITY POLITICS *See* City Government

Subheading ···· CITY PROBLEMS

        Problems and Solutions

        Build an Airport or a Train Depot? E. Citta. *The City Architect*

Author of Article ···· 85:44+ Mr '99

        Parking Lots Versus Green Parks. M. Kline. *The Neighborhood*

Volume and page numbers ···· *Gardener* 12: 5–6 Dec '01

▶ Search Online

An online search allows you to search a computer database to locate information. For example, you could find the names of local newspapers. Select a keyword to identify the topic you need to search. If you don't have success with the first keyword you try, you may need to broaden or narrow your search to find the information you require.

▶ Use Your Research

Place the new information from your research into the problem and solution organizer. This writer learned something and modified her organizer to include the new information. What change did she make?

> Alternative:
> Keep the park
>
> Benefits:
> 1. Good place for kids
> 2. Space for working together
> 3. Cool, relaxing area
> 4. Adds beauty
>
> Alternative:
> Build a parking lot
>
> Benefits:
> 1. Convenience for a few car owners
> 2. Income for parking lot operators
>
> Solution: Make everyone aware of the problem
> Write to the editor of the Globe

Checklist ✔

Research and Inquiry

- ■ Did you list your questions?
- ■ Did you figure out possible resources?
- ■ Did you take notes from your resources?

PRACTICE AND APPLY

Review Your Plan

1. Review your problem and solution organizer.

2. List questions you have about your topic.

3. Identify the resources that will help you answer them.

4. Add the new information you gather to your organizer.

5. Use the Research and Inquiry checklist.

Draft

Writing PROCESS

Before you begin writing your persuasive piece, look at the chart you made. Think about making a paragraph for each main idea. Include the details that support each main idea.

PROBLEM AND SOLUTION CHART

Main idea for first paragraph: State the problem.

Problem:
Community park is being turned into a parking lot

Main idea for second paragraph: Benefits of each alternative

Alternative: Keep the park

Alternative: Build a parking lot

Benefits:
1. Good place for kids
2. Space for working together
3. Cool, relaxing area
4. Adds beauty

Benefits:
1. Convenience for a few car owners
2. Income for parking lot operators

Solution: Make everyone aware of the problem
Write to the editor of the Globe

I will restate my opinions in the last paragraph.

✓ Checklist

Drafting

- Does your writing fit your purpose and audience?

- Have you included your opinions?

- Have you included details to support your argument?

- Do your word choices influence your reader?

- Do you have a strong ending for your piece?

Notice how this writer used the ideas from her chart to write a first draft of a letter to a newspaper. She presented the problem and her opinion in her first paragraph. She gave reasons to support her opinions and influence the reader.

PREWRITE

DRAFT

REVISE

PROOFREAD

PUBLISH

DRAFT

Dear Editor

People want to turn a vacant lot near my apartment building into a parking lot. We have been planting greenery in it for years. For many people in our area a park is more useful than a parking lot.

> *Clearly states opinion about the topic.*

Here are the benefits of each one. First, greenery makes a neighborhood nice. also, people from one to ninety one can enjoy a park. It is a good place for children to play and a space for the community to work together. The parking lot will benefit only car owners. It will also benefit the lot operators. As a concrete space it won't never match a garden.

> *Offers strong argument to support opinion.*

It is obvious that a green park is a much more valueable choice than another parking lot. Please print my letter so others will be aware of the issue.

> *Concluding paragraph emphatically restates opinion.*

PRACTICE AND APPLY
Draft Your Own Persuasive Piece

1. Review your prewriting organizer.

2. State your opinions, and give supporting reasons.

3. Use strong words that will influence your readers.

4. Put your reasons in a logical order.

TECHNOLOGY
Review your draft for logical order. Do the ideas flow smoothly? If not, try moving paragraphs or sentences around by cutting and pasting text.

Revise

Elaborate

One way to improve your writing is to elaborate. When you elaborate, you add important ideas and details that might be missing from your writing. When you revise your persuasive writing, pay attention to the details you use that will influence your readers to agree with your opinions.

The details the writer added clarify whom the reader should hold responsible for what the writer believes is a poor decision.

> *Town leaders*
> ~~People~~ want to turn a vacant lot near my apartment
> building into a parking lot.

The writer added the negative image of a bare parking lot and a positive description of the garden in an attempt to influence her readers.

> *bare*   *the beauty of*
> As a concrete space it won't never match a garden.

Word Choice

When you are writing, it is important to select the right words for your topic and audience.

In a persuasive piece, select words carefully to influence the opinion of your audience. This writer added opinion words and phrases to firmly establish her own opinion.

> *We ought to weigh*   *everybody agrees that*
> ~~Here are~~ the benefits of each one. First, greenery
> makes a neighborhood nice.

OPINION WORDS

must
should
I believe
everybody agrees
best
ought
never
always
everyone knows
truly

Better Sentences

As you revise your draft, focus on your sentences to make sure they work together well. Read your sentences aloud. How do they sound? Do your sentences flow smoothly? You may need to add transition words between ideas.

If your sentences are choppy but contain related ideas, combine them to make a more interesting sentence.

PREWRITE

DRAFT

REVISE

PROOFREAD

PUBLISH

> On the other hand,
> The parking lot will benefit only car owners. ~~It will also~~ *and*
> ~~benefit~~ the lot operators.

PRACTICE AND APPLY

Revise Your Own Persuasive Writing

1. Decide what details you can add to strengthen your argument.

2. Add opinion words that will try to convince your readers to agree with you.

3. **Grammar** Should you combine any sentences to make your writing read more smoothly?

TECHNOLOGY

Don't worry too much about making your work perfect when writing a first draft on the computer. Instead, focus on getting your ideas down, not on fixing all spelling or typing errors.

Revise • Peer Conferencing

Writing PROCESS

You have focused on your opinions in your persuasive writing. Now it's time to consider someone else's opinions. Exchange drafts with a partner. See what helpful ideas you can gain.

This can be more persuasive if you make "We" more specific.

Add more specific details to make arguments more convincing.

This makes a good ending.

Dear Editor

People want to turn a vacant lot near my apartment building into a parking lot. We have been planting greenery in it for years. For many people in our area a park is more useful than a parking lot.

Here are the benefits of each one. First, greenery makes a neighborhood nice. also, people from one to ninety one can enjoy a park. It is a good place for children to play and a space for the community to work together. The parking lot will benefit only car owners. It will also benefit the lot operators. As a concrete space it won't never match a garden.

It is obvious that a green park is a much more valueable choice than another parking lot. Please print my letter so others will be aware of the issue.

Conferencing for the Reader

■ Are features of persuasive writing included in your partner's piece?
- clear opinions
- convincing reasons and arguments
- logical order
- strongest argument is last
- opinion words

■ Tell your partner what's good about her or his writing as well as what needs improvement.

When you revise your persuasive writing, take into consideration the suggestions your partner shared. This writer made some changes based on her partner's ideas.

REVISE

The Boston Globe Editorial Department
Dear Editor   P.O. Box 55819
Town leaders   Boston MA 02205-5819

455 Park St.
Boston MA 02214
May 5, 2009

~~People~~ want to turn a vacant lot near my apartment
My community has   tending a garden
building into a parking lot. ~~We have been planting~~

~~greenery~~ in it for years. For many people in our area a

park is more useful than a parking lot.
         We ought to weigh   everybody agrees that
~~Here are~~ the benefits of each one. First, greenery
     adds beauty to any
~~makes a~~ neighborhood ~~nice~~. also, people from one to
                         The park is a safe
ninety one can enjoy a park. ~~It is a good~~ place for

children to play and a space for the community to work
         On the other hand
together. The parking lot will benefit only car owners. ~~It~~
              and   bare
~~will also benefit~~ the lot operators. As a concrete space it
         the beauty of
won't never match a garden.

   It is obvious that a green park is a much more
                         yet
valueable choice than another parking lot. Please print

my letter so others will be aware of the issue.
                         Yours Truly,
                         Lisa O'Brien

Revising

- Does your writing suit your purpose and audience?
- Does any of your writing need elaboration?
- Have you expressed your opinion clearly and forcefully?
- Did you use opinion words?
- Do your sentences flow smoothly when you read them aloud?

PRACTICE AND APPLY

Plan Your Own Persuasive Writing

1. Read your draft aloud, or have your partner read it.

2. Take notes from your partner's comments.

3. Use the notes from your peer conference to help make your draft better.

4. If your draft is a business letter, check to see that you have included all the parts.

Proofread/Edit

After you have revised your persuasive writing, you will need to proofread and edit it to find and correct any errors in mechanics, grammar and usage, and spelling.

STRATEGIES FOR PROOFREADING

- **Reread your revised paper.** Each time, look for a different type of error. You'll have a much better chance of catching all errors.

- **Read each sentence.** Make sure all first words and proper nouns are capitalized.

- **Reread for proper punctuation.** Use commas, colons, and hyphens correctly.

- **Check for spelling errors.** Focus on each word individually.

Spelling

When words end in silent *e*, drop the *e* when adding an ending that begins with a vowel, as in *value* and *valuable*.

REVIEW THE RULES

GRAMMAR

- Correct a double negative by removing one negative word or replacing one negative word with a positive word.

MECHANICS

- Use a comma after a long introductory prepositional phrase or after the last in a series of phrases.

- Use a colon between the hour and minute in time, to introduce a list of items, and after the greeting of a business letter.

- Use a hyphen in numbers, in some compound words, and to show the division of a word.

Go to pages 138–173 to review other rules.

Writing PROCESS

Look at the proofreading corrections made on the draft below. What does the symbol ⑤℗ mean? What spelling correction does the writer need to make?

PROOFREADING

The Boston Globe Editorial Department   455 Park St.
Dear Editor : P.O. Box 55819   Boston, MA 02214
Town leaders   Boston, MA 02205-5819   May 5, 2009

People want to turn a vacant lot near my apartment
                My community has   tending a garden
building into a parking lot. We have been planting

greenery in it for years. For many people in our area, a

park is more useful than a parking lot.
       We ought to weigh   everybody agrees that
Here are the benefits of each one. First, greenery
adds beauty to any
makes a neighborhood nice. also, people from one to
                                ≡ The park is a safe
ninety one can enjoy a park. It is a good place for

children to play and a space for the community to work
         On the other hand,
together. The parking lot will benefit only car owners. It
              and   bare
will also benefit the lot operators. As a concrete space, it
will   the beauty of
won't never match a garden.

    It is obvious that a green park is a much more
⑤℗ valuable   yet
valueable choice than another parking lot. Please print

my letter so others will be aware of the issue.   Yours Truly,
                                                   Lisa O'Brien

Checklist ✔

Proofreading

- Did you spell all words correctly?

- Did every sentence begin with a capital letter?

- Did you indent all paragraphs?

- Did you use commas correctly?

PROOFREADING MARKS

⌗ new paragraph

∧ add

ℒ take out

≡ Make a capital letter.

╱ Make a small letter.

⑤℗ Check the spelling.

⊙ Add a period.

PRACTICE AND APPLY

Proofread Your Own Persuasive Writing

1. Correct spelling errors.

2. Check capitalization.

3. Indent all paragraphs.

4. Make sure commas are used properly.

Publish

Before you publish your piece, review it one final time. Use a checklist to focus your final review.

✓ **Self-Check** **Persuasive Writing**

- ❑ Who was my audience? Will my writing influence them?
- ❑ What was my purpose? Will I persuade my reader to agree with me?
- ❑ Did I state my opinions clearly?
- ❑ Did I use opinion words to influence my reader?
- ❑ Was I careful to avoid double negatives?
- ❑ Did I present my arguments in a logical way?
- ❑ Did I save my strongest argument for last?
- ❑ Did I proofread and correct all errors?

The writer used the checklist to review her persuasive piece. Read her letter and respond to it in your journal. Did the writer persuade you to agree with her? Why do you think so?

455 Park St.
Boston, MA 02214
May 5, 2009

The Boston Globe Editorial Department
P.O. Box 55819
Boston, MA 02205-5819

Dear Editor:

Town leaders want to turn a vacant lot near my apartment building into a parking lot. My community has been tending a garden in it for years. For many people in our area, a park is more useful than a parking lot.

We ought to weigh the benefits of each one. First, everybody agrees that greenery adds beauty to any neighborhood. Also, people from one to ninety-one can enjoy a park. The park is a safe place for children to play and a space for the community to work together. On the other hand, the parking lot will benefit only car owners and the lot operators. As a bare concrete space, it will never match the beauty of a garden.

It is obvious that a green park is a much more valuable choice than yet another parking lot. Please print my letter so others will be aware of this issue.

Yours truly,

Lisa O'Brien

TECHNOLOGY

Many word processing programs provide a thesaurus. Learn how to use this feature so that you can add variety to your language.

PRACTICE AND APPLY

Publish Your Own Persuasive Writing

1. Check your revised draft a final time.

2. Make a neat final copy.

3. Include all parts if your writing is in letter form.

Persuasive Writing

Score	Description
4 Excellent	■ presents a focused, engaging text with a clearly argued opinion ■ uses a carefully planned sequence ■ shows a keen interest in the topic ■ uses challenging and precise words that are convincing ■ uses a variety of sentence types that flow smoothly ■ is free or almost free of errors
3 Good	■ presents a clear opinion with logical supporting details ■ has a clear beginning and ending with good transitions ■ uses a persuasive, personal tone ■ shows an effort to include persuasive language ■ uses mostly easy-to-follow sentences of different lengths ■ has minor errors that do not confuse the reader
2 Fair	■ states an unfocused opinion with weak supporting details ■ presents opinions and arguments in an order that does not flow ■ presents message but does not connect with readers ■ uses limited vocabulary with some errors ■ uses simple sentences that readers may need to reread ■ makes frequent errors that confuse the reader
1 Unsatisfactory	■ does not present a clear opinion ■ has no clear beginning or ending and no logical order ■ has a flat tone that does not persuade readers ■ uses vague and inappropriate words ■ uses incomplete and confusing sentences ■ makes serious and repeated errors

Go to www.macmillanmh.com for a 6-Point Student Writing Rubric.

Unit **3**
Fictional Narrative: A Story

Fictional Narrative: A Story

A story is a narrative that comes from the writer's imagination. It has a beginning, middle, and end. The story includes characters that move the action along. The setting, plot, and dialogue are important components in developing a story to hold the reader's attention.

Learning from Writers

Read the following examples of fictional narrative. Are the characters developed so that they move the story along? As you read, look for dialogue between characters that makes you feel that you are a part of the story.

THINK AND WRITE

Purpose
Why do you think people write stories? Write a brief explanation in your journal.

Rumpelstiltskin's Daughter

At the first cottage they came to, they asked to see granny. She hobbled to the door in her rags and curtsied to the king.

"Now," whispered Rumpelstiltskin's daughter, "give her a bag of wool and a pair of needles. Tell her to knit it all up and you will come back in a month to collect your riches. Give her a gold coin for her pains."

"Do I have to?" the king whined.

"My grandfather always did," she said. "I would, if I were you."

And so they went all over the kingdom, hiring every granny they could find.

At the end of the month, the king ordered his coach and wagons, rounded up his guards, and went to see the grannies. As he neared the first cottage, he heard the sound of singing. Looking out the window, the king saw the happy villagers waiting there to greet him, cheering wildly as he passed. And every one of them was warm as toast in yellow woolly clothes.

"Gold!" cried the king.

—Diane Stanley, from *Rumpelstiltskin's Daughter*

Getting Ready for the Big Day

"Get up, Linda. Your team is waiting for your practice run," called Linda's mother.

"Can't do it," said Linda yawning. "Too tired." She got up anyway. Today she knew she had to decide who would run the last leg.

Seated on the front porch were Tamara, Sally, and Lee—members of the relay team no one thought would win. This year, they planned to prove the nonbelievers at Calhoun Middle School wrong!

"Well, let's get going," Tamara urged. For the first practice run, Lee took the last leg. Her time was excellent.

"What do you think, Linda?" asked Lee.

Linda looked at her. Lee was the fastest, but she was not consistent. This morning, Linda decided to have faith. "It's yours," she replied. "Now, let's do it again."

—Lauren Freeman

PRACTICE AND APPLY

Thinking Like a Reader

1. Summarize the story from *Rumpelstiltskin's Daughter*.

2. What is Linda's response when her mother tries to wake her?

Thinking Like a Writer

3. How did the author of *Rumpelstiltskin's Daughter* bring the story to an end?

4. What dialogue words did the author use in "Getting Ready for the Big Day"?

5. **Reading Across Texts** Compare the two literature models. Write about the setting and the characters in each story.

Features of Fictional Narrative

DEFINITIONS AND FEATURES

A **fictional narrative** is a story that a writer creates from his or her imagination. A good story:

► Has an interesting **beginning, middle**, and **end**.

► Has a **plot** with a problem that is solved at the end.

► Describes a **setting**, telling where and when the story takes place.

► Can use **dialogue words** to vary the speaker's responses.

► Beginning, Middle, and End

Reread *Rumpelstiltskin's Daughter* by Diane Stanley on page 48. The beginning of a story usually introduces the characters and the problem. The middle of the story leads to a climax, a turning point. The end of the story shows the resolution to the problem, or the moral of the story. Read the passage below.

> . . . And every one of them was warm as toast in yellow woolly clothes.
>
> "Gold!" cried the king.

How does the author end the story of *Rumpelstiltskin's Daughter*?

► Characters

The characters are people in the story. Their actions create the plot.

> "Do I have to?" the king whined.
>
> "My grandfather always did," she said. "I would if I were you."

In this passage, what does the author show us about the personality of each of these characters?

▶ Plot

The plot is the sequence of events that take place in a story. Most plots revolve around a problem that is solved by the end of the story.

> "Now," whispered Rumpelstiltskin's daughter, "give her a bag of wool and a pair of needles. Tell her to knit it all and you will come back in a month to collect your riches. Give her a gold coin for her pains."

What problem might the king be experiencing? What problem might the people in the village have?

▶ Setting

The time and place of a story is the setting. The setting can be realistic or imaginary.

> And they went all over the kingdom, hiring every granny they could find.

▶ Dialogue Words

The dialogue holds the reader's attention by engaging them in the conversation. Dialogue words should vary throughout the story. Use words such as *murmured*, *stammered*, *cried*, *exclaimed*, *shouted*, *whispered*, *babbled*, *remarked*, *whined*, and *questioned*.

> "Now," whispered Rumpelstiltskin's daughter, "give her a bag of wool and a pair of needles."

How does the dialogue word in the above passage hold the reader's attention?

PRACTICE AND APPLY

Create a Beginning, Middle, and End Chart

1. Reread "Getting Ready for the Big Day" on page 49.
2. In the chart, write the events that took place at the beginning, middle, and end of the story.

Beginning	Middle	End

Prewrite

Writing PROCESS

A fictional narrative is a story written from a writer's imagination. Stories have a plot with a beginning, a middle, and an end. They also have a problem that a character solves. For your story, you can use make-believe characters from the past, the present, or the future. You can also use a setting that is a real or an imaginary time and place.

Purpose and Audience

The purpose of writing a story is to entertain your readers, or audience. Before you write your story, you need to think about who you are writing for. Your audience can be your teacher, your classmates, your family, or even yourself.

Choose a Topic

Start by **brainstorming** a list of ideas that might be developed into an interesting story. Then choose a topic.

After choosing a topic for your story, **explore ideas** by making a list of events. Also list the character's problem and how he or she may solve it. Later, you will organize these ideas.

THINK AND WRITE

Audience

In your journal, write how you would choose a topic that will make an interesting story for your audience.

Here are my ideas for my story.

Mayflower Journey

Sailed to New England
Ship sailed through violent storms
People got sick
Lots of people on board
Helped one another stay alive
Mother almost died
Boy solved the problem
Some people survived
Reached New England

Organize • Plot

A story has a beginning, a middle, and an end. This sequence of events is called a plot. When a story is based on historical events, the most important events should be arranged in chronological, or time, order. What ideas from his list did this writer leave out in this time line?

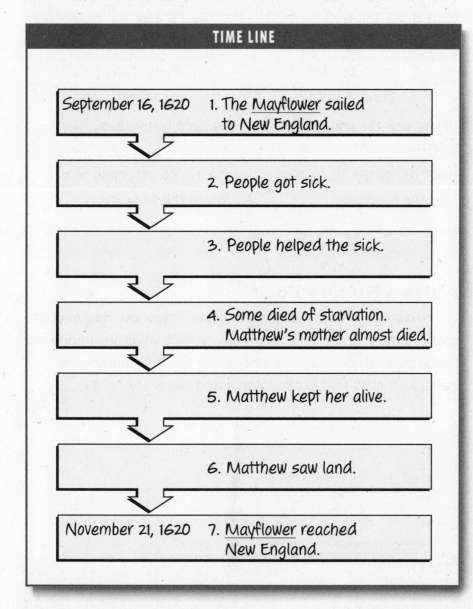

TIME LINE

September 16, 1620   1. The <u>Mayflower</u> sailed to New England.

2. People got sick.

3. People helped the sick.

4. Some died of starvation. Matthew's mother almost died.

5. Matthew kept her alive.

6. Matthew saw land.

November 21, 1620   7. <u>Mayflower</u> reached New England.

Checklist ✓
Prewriting

- Have you thought about your purpose and audience?

- Have you listed ideas for interesting stories?

- Have you chosen a topic and explored ideas about it?

- Are the events organized in a time line?

- Is there a beginning, a middle, and an end?

- Does your story have a plot, characters, and a setting?

- Do you need to research your topic?

PRACTICE AND APPLY

Plan Your Own Story

1. Think about your purpose and audience.

2. Brainstorm ideas that can be developed into a good story.

3. Choose a story topic and explore ideas.

4. Organize your ideas into a plot.

Prewrite • Research and Inquiry

Writing PROCESS

▶ Writer's Resources

You may have to do research to get more information for your fictional narrative. First, make a list of questions. Then decide what resources you will need to answer your questions.

What Else Do I Need to Know?	Where Can I Find the Information?
Where was the ship coming from?	Look in a history book.
What did people do to survive on the Mayflower?	Watch a documentary film about the Mayflower.

▶ Use a History Book

A history book is a reference resource you can find in your school library. It contains factual records of what has happened in the past. To find out if the book has the information you need, look at the table of contents and the index.

Use the table of contents to find out if your topic is listed and on what page it begins.

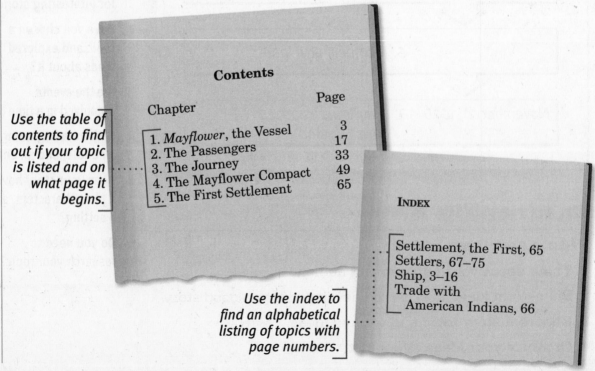

Contents

Chapter	Page
1. *Mayflower*, the Vessel	3
2. The Passengers	17
3. The Journey	33
4. The Mayflower Compact	49
5. The First Settlement	65

INDEX

Use the index to find an alphabetical listing of topics with page numbers.

► **Watch a Documentary**

A documentary is a movie that presents factual historical events. Look for specific details in the movie that will help you describe the setting and the characters more clearly. Write a summary to help you remember details to use in your story.

► **Use Your Research**

New information that you gathered from your research can be placed in your time line. This writer found important information from reading the history book. How did the time line change?

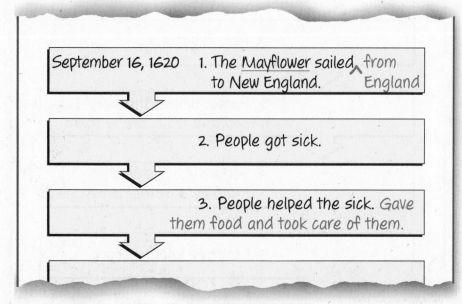

September 16, 1620   1. The Mayflower sailed ^from
                         to New England.   England

2. People got sick.

3. People helped the sick. Gave them food and took care of them.

PRACTICE AND APPLY

Review Your Plan

1. Look at your time line.

2. List questions that you have about your topic.

3. Identify the resources that you will need to gather information.

4. Add new information that you gathered to your time line.

55

Draft

Before you can begin writing your story, you need to review your time line. Think about making a new paragraph for each main idea. You should include details to support each main idea.

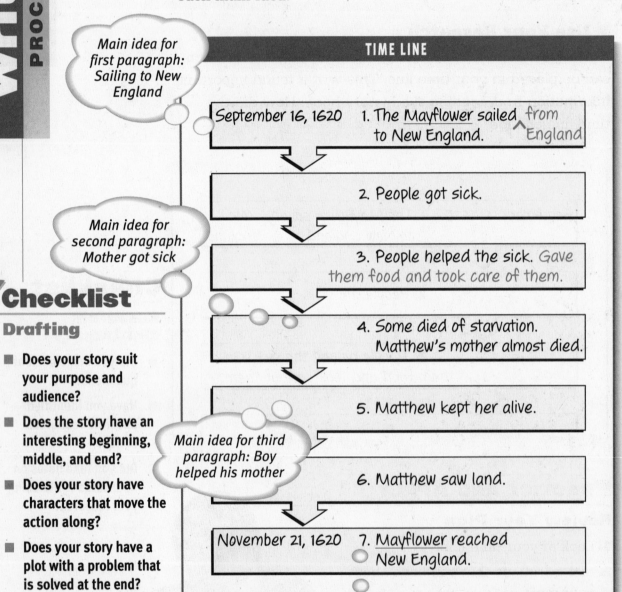

Main idea for first paragraph: Sailing to New England

Main idea for second paragraph: Mother got sick

Main idea for third paragraph: Boy helped his mother

I can use this idea to end the story.

TIME LINE

September 16, 1620 — 1. The Mayflower sailed to New England. *from England*

2. People got sick.

3. People helped the sick. *Gave them food and took care of them.*

4. Some died of starvation. Matthew's mother almost died.

5. Matthew kept her alive.

6. Matthew saw land.

November 21, 1620 — 7. Mayflower reached New England.

✓ Checklist

Drafting

- Does your story suit your purpose and audience?

- Does the story have an interesting beginning, middle, and end?

- Does your story have characters that move the action along?

- Does your story have a plot with a problem that is solved at the end?

- Does the story have a setting that tells when and where the action takes place?

- Is dialogue used to make your characters come alive?

Look at how the writer used the ideas in his time line to write his first draft. He elaborated about the journey on the *Mayflower*. He related a problem and how one of the characters solved it.

DRAFT

Years ago, people left home to find a new life. Among them were a young boy named Matthew and his family. They left England on the <u>Mayflower</u> on September 16, 1620, to sail to New England.

Setting and characters

On the third week, people got sick. Some died from lack of food. Matthew's mother almost died. He knew he had to help her.

Problem to be solved

The children were fed first. Matthew always got some food. He would eat a little and hide some food. Then he took the food to his mother. Here mother. I saved this for you," he said. "You are a wonderful boy, Matthew. Thank you" she said.

Supporting details tell how the boy helped his mother

Ending or conclusion of story

His mother regained her strength. Matthew saw land. On November 21, 1620, the <u>Mayflower</u> sailed into Massachusetts, where a new life awayted he and his family.

PRACTICE AND APPLY

Draft Your Own Story

1. Review your prewriting time line.
2. Write about your character.
3. Events should be in the order in which they occurred.

TECHNOLOGY

The most important thing is to get your ideas typed on the computer. Remember, your first draft does not have to be perfect. You will have an opportunity to go back and make corrections later.

Revise

Elaborate

One way to improve your story is to elaborate. This means adding important ideas and details about the setting, characters, and plot to give a better explanation of the problem and how it is solved.

This writer added details about the characters to help the reader visualize them.

> *an eleven-year-old*
> Among them were a ~~young~~ boy named Matthew
> *mother and father*
> and his ~~family~~. They left England on the <u>Mayflower</u>
> on September 16, 1620, to sail to New England.

DIALOGUE WORDS

said

asked

replied

answered

exclaimed

remarked

commented

whispered

Word Choice

Choose words that are right for your topic and audience. You need to find words that will vary the speaker's responses when dialogue is being spoken. This makes the story more interesting.

> Then he took the food to his mother. Here mother. I
> *whispered.*
> saved this for you," he ~~said.~~ "You are a wonderful boy,
> *replied*
> Matthew. Thank you" she ~~said.~~

Better Paragraphs

Look closely at each paragraph. Make sure that all the sentences work together. If a sentence does not help to clarify the theme, rewrite it or delete it.

Use transition words to connect ideas. Add time-order transitions, such as *next* and *then,* to help your plot flow from one event to the next.

> From then on, Finally, in late October,
> ∧His mother regained her strength. Matthew saw land.∧

PRACTICE AND APPLY

Revise Your Own Story

1. Clarify what you have already said by including more details or information.

2. Try to say new things in each paragraph, being careful not to repeat what has already been said.

3. **Grammar** Have you used vivid action verbs and dialogue words correctly?

TECHNOLOGY

Revising on the computer takes a short amount of time. To erase something, highlight it by using the mouse. Then use the delete key to remove the writing. If you need to add details, put the cursor where you want to insert the new information. Then type in the information.

Revise • Peer Conferencing

When you finish your draft, step back from your writing and get a new point of view. To do so, ask a partner to read your draft and make suggestions for improvement. In turn, read your partner's writing.

Add details for a better beginning.

Years ago, people left home to find a new life. Among them were a young boy named Matthew and his family. They left England on the <u>Mayflower</u> on September 16, 1620, to sail to New England.

Sentences are choppy. Revise for better flow.

On the third week, people got sick. Some died from lack of food. Matthew's mother almost died. He knew he had to help her.

Make these sentences more vivid.

The children were fed first. Matthew always got some food. He would eat a little and hide some food. Then he took the food to his mother. Here mother. I saved this for you," he said. "You are a wonderful boy, Matthew. Thank you" she said.

Dialogue makes me feel as if I were there.

His mother regained her strength. Matthew saw land. On November 21, 1620, the <u>Mayflower</u> sailed into Massachusetts, where a new life awaited he and his family.

Conferencing for the Reader

■ Are features of a story included in your partner's piece?
  • beginning, middle, and end
  • characters that move the story along
  • plot with a problem that is solved at the end
  • setting that tells where and when the story takes place
  • dialogue words
■ Be sure to tell what is good about the piece.

When you revise your story, you will want to consider the comments and suggestions that your peer conferencing partner gave you. This writer made some changes based on his partner's ideas.

PREWRITE

DRAFT

REVISE

PROOFREAD

PUBLISH

REVISE

Nearly four hundred ∧ crossed the seas
Years ago, people left home to find a new life.
an eleven-year-old
Among them were a young boy named Matthew and
mother and father
his family. They left England on the Mayflower on

September 16, 1620, to sail to New England.
During   of the journey   began to die
On the third week, people got sick. Some died
was among the starving, and
from lack of food. Matthew's mother almost died.

He knew he had to help her.
Since
The children were fed first, Matthew always got
take a few bites   in his pocket
some food. He would eat a little and hide some food.
when everyone was asleep,
Then he took the food to his mother. Here mother.
whispered
I saved this for you," he said. "You are a wonderful
replied
boy, Matthew. Thank you" she said.
From then on,   Finally, in late October,
His mother regained her strength. Matthew saw

land. On November 21, 1620, the Mayflower sailed

into Massachusetts, where a new life awaited he

and his family.

Checklist ✓
Revising

- Does your story fit your purpose and audience?

- Do you need to elaborate on any part of your story? Have you included enough details about the characters and the setting?

- Is there dialogue to make your story more interesting?

- Do you have an interesting beginning, middle, and end?

- Do your sentences flow well when you read your story aloud?

PRACTICE AND APPLY

Revise Your Own Story

1. Read your draft aloud. Listen carefully to how your story sounds.

2. Take notes from your peer conference.

3. Use your partner's comments to help make your draft better.

Writing PROCESS

Proofread/Edit

Now that you have revised your story, you will need to proofread it. Proofreading will allow you to find and correct any errors in mechanics, grammar and usage, and spelling.

STRATEGIES FOR PROOFREADING

- **Reread your revised story.** Look for a different type of error each time. This will help you catch all errors.

- **Read each sentence for correct punctuation and capitalization.** Check commas and quotation marks.

- **Reread to check for correct subject-verb agreement.**

- **Check for spelling errors.** Use your finger to slowly follow each word of the story in order to focus on one word at a time.

Spelling
Look for word chunks or smaller words that help you remember the spelling of the word, for example: *May + flower = Mayflower*.

REVIEW THE RULES

GRAMMAR

- A verb must agree with its subject. The ending may change depending on which or how many people or things do the action. The tense of a verb tells whether the action takes place in the present, past, or future.

MECHANICS

- Use quotation marks before and after a direct quotation.

- A quotation begins with a capital letter. If a quoted sentence is broken up by the name of the speaker, the second part of the sentence is not capitalized.

- When the speaker changes, begin a new paragraph.

- Use a comma to set off the speaker from the spoken words when the speaker is named before the quotation. Use a question mark, exclamation point, or comma when the speaker is named after the quotation. Place end punctuation inside the quotation marks.

Go to pages 138–173 to review other rules.

Look at the proofreading corrections made on the draft below. What does the symbol ⌗ mean? Why does the writer start a new paragraph?

PROOFREAD

Nearly four hundred   crossed the seas
Years ago, people left home to find a new life.
                an eleven-year-old
Among them were a young boy named Matthew and
        mother and father
his family. They left England on the Mayflower on

September 16, 1620, to sail to New England.
    During   of the journey   began to die
On the third week, people got sick. Some died
                    was among the starving, and
from lack of food. Matthew's mother almost died.

He knew he had to help her.
    Since
The children were fed first, Matthew always got
            take a few bites   in his pocket
some food. He would eat a little and hide some food.
,when everyone was asleep,
Then he took the food to his mother. Here, mother.
                    whispered ⌗
I saved this for you," he said. "You are a wonderful
                        replied
boy, Matthew. Thank you", she said.
From then on,   Finally, in late October,
His mother regained her strength. Matthew saw

land. On November 21, 1620, the Mayflower sailed
                            (SP)
into Massachusetts, where a new life awayted he
and his family.

PRACTICE AND APPLY

Proofread Your Own Story

1. Correct spelling mistakes.

2. Check subject-verb agreement.

3. Correct punctuation and capitalization errors.

4. Check for correct use of quotation marks.

Checklist ✓
Proofreading

- Did you indent your paragraphs?

- Did you spell each word correctly?

- Which punctuation errors do you need to correct?

- Did you begin every sentence with a capital letter?

- Did you look for subject-verb agreement?

- Have you used quotation marks correctly?

PROOFREADING MARKS

⌗   new paragraph

∧   add

℘   take out

≡   Make a capital letter.

/   Make a small letter.

(SP)   Check the spelling.

⊙   Add a period.

Publish

You are almost ready to publish! Before you do so, you need to review your writing one last time. Using a checklist can help guide your efforts.

✓ Self-Check   A Story

- ❑ Who was my audience? Did I write to entertain them?
- ❑ Did I grab my audience's attention at the beginning of my story?
- ❑ Does my story have a strong middle and an end?
- ❑ Did I include details so that the writing was clear to the reader?
- ❑ Did I vary my dialogue words?
- ❑ Did the sentences flow well?
- ❑ Do my subjects and verbs agree?
- ❑ Did I proofread and correct all mistakes?

The writer used the checklist to review his story. Read "Matthew's Journey" and discuss it in a small group. Do you think the story was ready to be published? Why do you think so?

Matthew's Journey
by Justin Walker

Nearly four hundred years ago, people crossed the seas to find a new life. Among them were an eleven-year-old named Matthew and his mother and father. They left England on the *Mayflower* on September 16, 1620, to sail to New England.

During the third week of the journey, people got sick. Some began to die from lack of food. Matthew's mother was among the starving, and he knew he had to help her.

Since the children were fed first, Matthew always got some food. He would take a few bites and hide some food in his pocket. Then, when everyone was asleep, he took the food to his mother. "Here, Mother. I saved this for you," he whispered.

"You are a wonderful boy, Matthew. Thank you," she replied.

From then on, his mother regained her strength. Finally, in late October, Matthew saw land. On November 21, 1620, the *Mayflower* sailed into Massachusetts, where a new life awaited him and his family.

PREWRITE

DRAFT

REVISE

PROOFREAD

PUBLISH

PRACTICE AND APPLY

Publish Your Own Story

1. Check your revised draft a final time.

2. Copy your revised draft over neatly or print a clean copy.

3. Include a map, chart, graph, or drawing in your story.

TECHNOLOGY

Add some clip art or other graphics to illustrate your story.

Fictional Narrative: A Story

Score	Description
4 Excellent	■ creates an entertaining story with specific characters and setting ■ has a focused narrative with an engaging beginning, middle, and end ■ expresses emotions and includes believable dialogue ■ uses rich language to create images and engaging dialogue ■ includes a variety of sentences that have rhythm and flow ■ is free or almost free of errors
3 Good	■ creates a solid story with characters and a realistic setting ■ has a well-planned plot with a clear beginning, middle, and end ■ uses an original voice and creates natural dialogue ■ uses a variety of both new and everyday words ■ uses mostly easy-to-follow sentences of different lengths ■ has minor errors that do not confuse the reader
2 Fair	■ tells a story but characters and setting are unclear ■ does not tie story events together or reach a conclusion ■ attempts to but does not engage or entertain the reader ■ uses ordinary words with some errors in usage ■ uses sentences that are mostly simple or short ■ makes frequent errors that confuse the reader
1 Unsatisfactory	■ creates a story that lacks details or setting ■ does not flow at all from beginning to end ■ does not attempt to appeal to readers ■ uses words in a confused or incorrect way ■ uses sentences that are incomplete or confusing ■ makes serious and repeated errors

Go to www.macmillanmh.com for a 6-Point Student Writing Rubric.

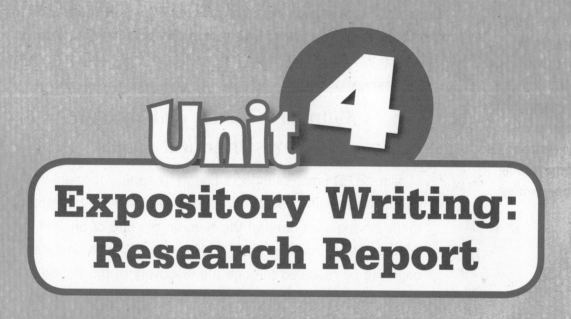

Unit 4
Expository Writing: Research Report

Expository Writing

When was the last time you gave important information about a specific topic? Your facts and details are an example of expository writing. This type of writing summarizes facts from different sources to draw a logical conclusion.

Learning from Writers

Read the following examples of expository writing. What facts and information do they present? As you read, look for the main idea and how the writers develop it with details.

THINK AND WRITE

Purpose
Why do you think people write to inform, explain, or report? Write a brief explanation in your journal. Also explain what you can learn from reading expository writing.

Mummies, Tombs, and Treasure: Secrets of Ancient Egypt

In 1875, unusual objects began to appear for sale in the shops, hotels, and bazaars of Luxor. This new city had sprung to life on the east bank of the Nile, on the site of ancient Thebes. Ever since the early 1800s, when Egypt's past had begun to be revealed through the discovery of the Rosetta Stone, the country had been swarming with foreign visitors. Among them were tourists, souvenir seekers, art collectors, and archaeologists, who were studying the monuments and digging for the remains of Egypt's ancient civilization.

The mysterious objects that were coming on the market turned out to be scrolls, *shabtis,* and other articles belonging to the various rulers of the New Kingdom and of the Twenty-first Dynasty, which followed it. Finally, in 1881, the Egyptian government tracked down the source of the articles. Sure enough, one of the old tomb-robbing families had been at work again. A pair of brothers had discovered the hiding place of the mummies near the temple of Queen Hatshepsut.

—Lila Perl, from *Mummies, Tombs, and Treasure: Secrets of Ancient Egypt*

An Ancient Inca City

There are many remarkable archaeological sites in the Western Hemisphere, but one of the most fascinating of all is Machu Picchu, a monument to the great civilizations of the Incas.

First of all, the Incas were talented architects who worked in stone. They did not use any form of mortar or cement to hold their buildings together. Instead, the Incan architects fitted stones together with such skill and precision that their buildings have stood for centuries.

Machu Picchu is home to the remains of about two hundred stone structures, including homes, meeting places, temples, and water storage receptacles. Many archaeologists believe that Machu Picchu was built as protection for the city of Cuzco, home of the Incan rulers.

–Anna Lopez

PRACTICE AND APPLY

Thinking Like a Reader

1. In which sentence does Anna Lopez state her main idea?

2. What important information did you learn about Machu Picchu from "An Ancient Inca City"?

Thinking Like a Writer

3. What details did the writer provide about the main idea?

4. How did the writer connect each piece of information in "An Ancient Inca City?"

5. **Reading Across Texts** Compare the two selections. What conclusions does each writer reach?

Expository Writing: Research Report

DEFINITIONS AND FEATURES

Expository writing, such as a research report, gives facts and information about a topic in an organized way. A good report:

▶ Introduces a **main idea** and develops it with facts and details.

▶ Gives **important information** about a specific topic.

▶ **Summarizes** information from a variety of different sources.

▶ Draws a **conclusion** based on the facts and information presented.

▶ Uses **transition words** to connect ideas.

▶ Main Idea

Reread Lila Perl's article on page 68. What do you think is the main idea of the passage?

> In 1875, unusual objects began to appear for sale in the shops, hotels, and bazaars of Luxor.

The writer states the main idea in the first sentence. When the writer says "unusual objects began to appear for sale," you know the passage will explain how these odd items reached the marketplace.

▶ Important Information

The writer provides key details about the topic. What details do you learn from this passage?

> The mysterious objects that were coming on the market turned out to be scrolls, *shabtis,* and other articles belonging to various rulers of the New Kingdom and of the Twenty-first Dynasty, which followed it.

These facts tell you that many people wanted antiques from Egypt's distant past.

▶ Summarizes from Different Sources

The writer draws information from many different sources to present a balanced and complete explanation.

> Ever since the early 1800s, when Egypt's past had begun to be revealed through the Rosetta Stone, the country had been swarming with foreign visitors.

What sources do you think were used for this summary?

▶ Draws a Conclusion

To help readers understand the explanation, the author pulls the facts and information together at the end.

> Sure enough, one of the old tomb-robbing families had been at work again. A pair of brothers had discovered the hiding place of the mummies near the temple of Queen Hatshepsut.

After presenting many different facts, the author comes up with a conclusion about the robberies. What were the brothers doing?

▶ Transition Words

To help your readers link ideas, you need to add *transitions*—words and phrases that show the relationship between ideas and events.

> Finally, in 1881, the Egyptian government tracked down the source of the articles.

What transition word did the writer use here?

PRACTICE AND APPLY

Create an Idea Web

1. List the features of an effective expository essay.
2. Reread "An Ancient Inca City" by Anna Lopez on page 69.
3. In each circle, write one example of each feature in the passage.
4. Write what you learned about Machu Picchu from the passage.

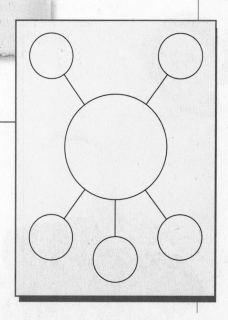

Prewrite

Expository writing gives facts and information about a particular topic. Writing a research report helps you find out more about a topic that interests you and lets you share that information with others.

Purpose and Audience

Expository essays explain information that your audience may want to know. As a way of explaining, expository essays summarize information from a variety of sources and draw conclusions based on the facts.

Start by thinking about what your audience may already know about your topic. Consider what new information you can present that your readers will find useful and interesting.

Choose a Topic

Begin by **brainstorming** a list of topics you would like to know more about. You might get ideas by thinking about your own interests or hobbies. Circle topics you think will also interest your audience.

Once you choose a topic, **explore ideas** by listing facts you know and questions you want to answer. Later, you will choose ideas from your list and organize them.

THINK AND WRITE

Audience
Make a report for first graders. How does it differ from a report written for readers your own age? Write down your thoughts.

I jotted down my ideas on note cards so that I could organize them later.

How do meteorologists predict tornadoes?
Use of radar

People watching tornadoes
Tornadoes destroy homes and injure people.

Tornadoes = cyclones, twisters
Tornadoes happen in spring and summer every year.

Organize • Classify

Expository essays introduce a main idea and develop it with facts and supporting details. First, look back at your note cards. Then, after crossing out ideas you do not plan to use, organize your ideas in a chart. How did the writer use an idea web to organize her ideas?

PREWRITE

DRAFT

REVISE

PROOFREAD

PUBLISH

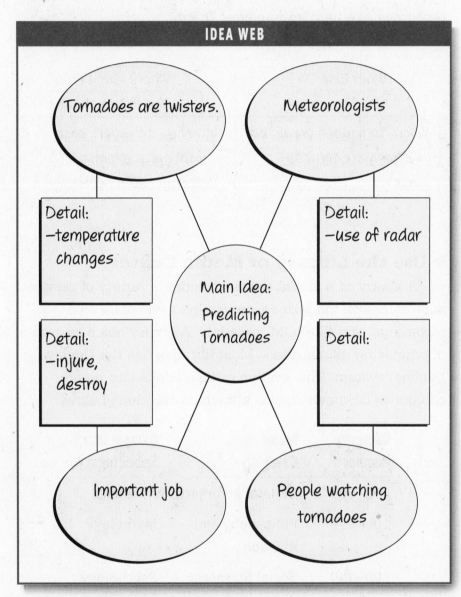

IDEA WEB

- Tornadoes are twisters.
- Meteorologists
- Detail:
  - —temperature changes
- Detail:
  - —use of radar
- Main Idea: Predicting Tornadoes
- Detail:
  - —injure, destroy
- Detail:
- Important job
- People watching tornadoes

Checklist ✓
Prewriting

- Have you listed interesting topics?

- Have you chosen a topic and brainstormed ideas about it?

- Have you analyzed your audience?

- Have you crossed off ideas that don't support the main idea?

- Are your ideas organized in a table?

- Do you know what facts you need to research?

PRACTICE AND APPLY

Plan Your Own Report

1. Think about your purpose for writing and your audience.

2. Brainstorm topic ideas.

3. Choose a topic and explore ideas.

4. Organize your ideas in a chart.

Writing PROCESS

Prewrite • Research and Inquiry

▶ Writer's Resources

To get the facts you need to support your main idea, you will need to do research. Look for gaps in information in your prewriting web. Write questions and decide which resources can help you answer them.

What Else Do I Need to Know?	Where Can I Find the Information?
How are tornadoes predicted? How strong are tornado winds?	Interview an expert, such as a local meteorologist. Visit the media center.

▶ Use the Library or Media Center

A library or a media center provides a variety of services, such as books, magazines, newspapers, videos, audio recordings, and CD-ROM materials. A library has a system of organizing its materials. Most libraries use the Dewey Decimal system. This system groups books into broad categories of knowledge as shown on the chart below.

A reference book such as an almanac, atlas, or encyclopedia will have a number between 000–099 on its spine.

A book about how meteorologists track tornadoes will have a number between 500–699 on its spine.

Category Number	Major Category	Sample of a Subcategory
000–099	General Reference	Almanacs
100–299	Philosophy and Religion	Mythology
300–399	Social Sciences	Psychology
400–499	Language	Spanish
500–699	Science, Mathematics, and Technology	Meteorology
700–899	Arts and Literature	Plays
900–999	Geography and History	American History

▶ Interview an Expert

Some meteorologists will be happy to be interviewed in person, on the telephone, or by e-mail. Whichever method you choose, prepare your questions. If you don't understand something, ask follow-up questions. Take complete notes. End the interview by thanking the expert. Write a thank-you note, too.

▶ Use Your Research

Add information you learn to your chart. How did the writer use new information to complete her idea web?

Tornadoes are twisters.
Tornado is Spanish word for "thunderstorm"

Meteorologists
—National Weather Service forecasters

Detail:
—temperature changes
—300 mph

Detail:
—use of radar
—Doppler

Main Idea:
Predicting Tornadoes

Detail:
—injure, destroy
—millions lost

Detail:
—Skywarn volunteers

Checklist ✔

Research and Inquiry

■ Did you write your questions ahead of time?

■ If an answer was unclear, did you ask more questions?

■ Did you save time by finding the most useful sources?

■ Did you take complete notes that include the names of your sources?

PRACTICE AND APPLY

Review Your Plan

1. Look for gaps in information in your idea web.

2. List questions that need an answer.

3. Think about what resources can give you the answer.

4. Add new information from your research.

Draft

Review your table carefully. See if you need to eliminate any information that does not support your main idea. Plan the order in which you will write your information. Give each main idea its own paragraph.

IDEA WEB

Main idea of second paragraph

Tornadoes are twisters.
Tornado is Spanish word for "thunderstorm"

Meteorologists
—National Weather Service forecasters

Detail:
—temperature changes
—300 mph

Detail:
—use of radar
—Doppler

Main Idea:
Predicting Tornadoes

Detail:
—injure, destroy
—millions lost

Detail:
—Skywarn volunteers

Important job

People watching tornadoes

Main idea of first paragraph

Details that support the idea of how forecasters track tornadoes

✓ Checklist

Drafting

- Does your report give your audience information they need or want?

- Did you find different sources to make sure your research is accurate?

- Did you state your main idea in your first paragraph?

- Do your middle paragraphs give facts and details that support your main idea?

- Did you draw a conclusion based on the information in your report?

How did the writer organize her ideas? First, she stated that predicting tornadoes is an important job. Then, she explained how forecasters do it. Finally, she drew a conclusion based on her facts.

DRAFT

Tornadoes cause injury and death to thousands of people and damage to millions of american homes every year, early warning is crucial. Predicting tornadoes is a important job. Tornado is the Spanish word for "thunderstorm."

— Main idea of report

The National Weather Service forecasters, such as Dr. Fields, do the job by watching weather conditions that often preced tornadoes. He explained that if these are present they use the Doppler radar to track down strong winds. However, this tool is often not enough. Some information also comes from weather watchers called Skywarn volunteers they gather data about the weather in their neighborhoods and pass them on. Predicting tornadoes is not an exact science. As meteorologists get more better more lives will be saved.

— Details describe how forecasters do the job.

— Conclusion

PRACTICE AND APPLY

Draft Your Own Report

1. State your main idea from your prewriting chart.

2. Organize your ideas into paragraphs.

3. Describe each idea with specific details.

4. Write a conclusion based on information in your report.

TECHNOLOGY

Make a header for your report that includes the date. That way, you can look through your hard copies and quickly see which version is the most recent.

Revise

Elaborate

One way to improve your writing is to *elaborate*. When you elaborate, you add important ideas and details that might be missing from your writing. As you revise your report, you may need to add details or examples to make your information clearer or more accurate.

The writer added details that tell more about weather conditions that may be used to predict a tornado.

> The National Weather Service forecasters, such as
> like thunderstorms and sudden temperature changes
> Dr. Fields, do the job by watching weather conditions,
>
> that often preced tornadoes.

Word Choice

Your reader's ability to follow the logic of your report will depend partly on the words you choose.

Transition words link ideas to help your audience understand how the ideas are related. Here, the writer will select transition words that show cause and effect.

> Fortunately,
> Predicting tornadoes is not an exact science. As
> are getting   at their job. As a result, in the future.
> meteorologists get more better more lives will be saved.

TRANSITION WORDS

after
although
as a result
however
in the first place
instead
similarly
therefore
though
unlike
when
yet

Better Sentences

Each time you revise, reread your sentences aloud. How do they sound? Does your writing sound boring because you haven't used vivid verbs and precise adjectives? Adding precise, vivid language will make your writing more exact and descriptive.

> He explained that if these are present ~~they use~~
> *in the atmosphere, meteorologists turn to*
> the Doppler radar to track down strong ^*swirling*^ winds.
> However, this tool is often not enough.
> ^*modern, powerful*^

PRACTICE AND APPLY

Revise Your Own Report

1. Add vivid verbs, precise adjectives, and words that appeal to the senses to make your writing more descriptive and interesting.

2. Choose words that express your ideas accurately and effectively.

3. Use transition words to show cause and effect.

4. **Grammar** Can you combine any sentences that have the same subjects, verbs, or other words?

TECHNOLOGY

When you revise, paste a new copy of the paragraph right below the original. Keep the original paragraph in view until you are satisfied with your revised paragraph. Then delete the original.

Revise • Peer Conferencing

Now, step back from your writing. Ask a partner to read your draft and make suggestions. Do the same to your partner's piece.

> This main-idea statement would make a good beginning.

> This sentence does not fit with the other ideas.

> This is not vivid enough. Elaborate by adding details.

> Good conclusion, but sentences need better transition.

Tornadoes cause injury and death to thousands of people and damage to millions of american homes every year, early warning is crucial. Predicting tornadoes is a important job. Tornado is the Spanish word for "thunderstorm."

The National Weather Service forecasters, such as Dr. Fields, do the job by watching weather conditions that often preced tornadoes. He explained that if these are present they use the Doppler radar to track down strong winds. However, this tool is often not enough. Some information also comes from weather watchers called Skywarn volunteers they gather data about the weather in their neighborhoods and pass them on. Predicting tornadoes is not an exact science. As meteorologists get more better more lives will be saved.

Conferencing for the Reader

■ Are the features of expository writing included in your partner's draft?
  • main idea
  • facts and details that explain the main idea
  • summary of information from different sources
  • conclusion
  • transitional words and phrases

■ Make sure to tell your partner what's good about the piece, as well as what needs improvement. Be constructive in your criticism.

Consider your partner's comments and revise your report based on them. Here is how this writer did it.

REVISE

Because
> Tornadoes cause injury and death to thousands of people and damage to millions of american homes every year, early warning is crucial. ~~Predicting tornadoes is a important job. Tornado is the Spanish word for "thunderstorm."~~

The National Weather Service forecasters, such as Dr. Fields, do the job by watching weather conditions *like thunderstorms and sudden temperature changes* that often preced tornadoes. He explained that if these are present, *in the atmosphere, meteorologists turn to* they use the Doppler radar to track down *swirling* strong winds. However, this *modern, powerful* tool is often not enough. Some information also comes from *a network of* weather watchers called Skywarn volunteers they gather *shifts in* data about the weather *conditions* in their neighborhoods and pass them on. Predicting tornadoes is not an exact science. *Fortunately,* As meteorologists *are getting* get more better *at their job.* more lives *As a result,* will be saved. *in the future*

PRACTICE AND APPLY

Revise Your Own Report

1. Ask a partner to comment on your draft.

2. Think about your partner's comments and decide how to use them to revise your report.

3. As you make each change, read your report aloud to see if the change flows smoothly.

4. Take out information from your draft that isn't necessary.

Checklist ✓

Revising

- Do the ideas in your report suit your purpose and audience?

- Can you elaborate on any of your ideas to make them clearer or more accurate?

- Do the facts and examples in your report appear in a logical order?

- Did you use transition words to show cause and effect?

- Did you add vivid verbs, precise adjectives, and sensory details?

- Did you choose your words carefully? Do all the sentences fit together well?

81

Proofread/Edit

Once you are satisfied that you have explained your ideas fully, you will need to proofread and edit your report to find and correct errors in mechanics, grammar and usage, and spelling.

STRATEGIES FOR PROOFREADING

- **Don't try to find all the errors in one reading.** Reread your report several times, focusing on a different type of error each time.

- **Make sure you have used articles correctly.** Look at the word that follows the article to determine which one to use.

- **Read your report aloud.** Make short pauses for commas and long pauses for periods to check punctuation.

- **Check for omitted or reversed letters.** Correct all spelling errors.

TECHNOLOGY

Make sure that you know how to use the spell checker. Remember that the spell checker will find only words that are misspelled, not words that are misused, such as *a* and *an*. As a result, you must proofread your work after you use a spell checker.

REVIEW THE RULES

GRAMMAR

- A pronoun takes the place of one or more nouns. Pronouns can be singular or plural and can be used as either subjects or objects in a sentence.

- Use the irregular comparative and superlative forms of *good* and *bad*: *better, best* and *worse, worst*.

- Use the article *a* before a word that starts with a consonant sound. Use the article *an* before a word that starts with a vowel sound.

MECHANICS

- Use abbreviations for dates, addresses, and people's titles.

Go to pages 138–173 to review other rules.

Writing PROCESS

Look at the proofreading corrections on the draft below. What does the symbol ∧ mean? What does the writer want to add? Why?

PROOFREAD

Because
∧Tornadoes cause injury and death to thousands of people and damage to millions of american homes every year, early warning is crucial. ~~Predicting tornadoes is a important job.~~ an ~~Tornado is the Spanish word for "thunderstorm."~~

The National Weather Service forecasters, such as
like thunderstorms and sudden temperature changes
Dr. Fields, do the job by watching weather conditions,∧
(sp)
that often ~~preced~~ tornadoes. He explained that if
in the atmosphere, meteorologists turn to
these are present ~~they use~~ the Doppler radar to track
, swirling   modern, powerful
down strong winds. However, this∧tool is often not.
a network of
enough. Some information also comes from∧weather
watchers called Skywarn volunteers∧they gather
shifts in   conditions
data about∧the weather∧in their neighborhoods and
#
pass them on. Predicting tornadoes is not an exact
Fortunately,   are getting   at their job. As a result,
science.∧As meteorologists ~~get more~~ better∧more lives
in the future
will be saved.∧

PRACTICE AND APPLY

Proofread Your Own Report

1. Correct spelling errors.

2. Make sure the articles *a* and *an* are used correctly.

3. Indent the beginning of each paragraph.

4. Correct any errors in capitalization and punctuation.

Checklist ✓
Proofreading

- Did you check that the articles *a* and *an* were used correctly?
- Did you use the proper form of pronouns?
- Did you check that all names and titles are capitalized?

PROOFREADING MARKS

#	new paragraph
∧	add
℘	take out
≡	Make a capital letter.
/	Make a small letter.
(sp)	Check the spelling.
⊙	Add a period.

83

Publish

Before publishing, check your report one last time. Use a checklist to help you focus on key elements.

✓ Self-Check Expository Writing

❑ **Did I keep my audience in mind while writing my report? Will my audience find my report interesting?**

❑ **Did I accomplish my purpose? Will my audience get useful information from my report?**

❑ **Did my introduction state my main idea clearly? Did I draw a conclusion based on the information in my report?**

❑ **Did I include an explanation that my audience will easily understand?**

❑ **Did I use transition words to connect ideas in my report?**

❑ **Did I use a variety of sentences to make my writing interesting?**

❑ **Did I proofread carefully and correct my errors?**

The writer used the checklist before publishing her report. Read "Predicting Tornadoes" and summarize the writer's points in your journal. Is the information useful? Is it written in a way you can easily understand?

Predicting Tornadoes
by Tamesha Woodruff

Predicting tornadoes is an important job. Because tornadoes cause injury and death to thousands of people and damage to millions of American homes every year, early warning is crucial.

The National Weather Service forecasters, such as Dr. Fields, do the job by watching weather conditions like thunderstorms and sudden temperature changes that often precede tornadoes. He explained that if these are present in the atmosphere, meteorologists turn to the Doppler radar to track down strong, swirling winds. However, this modern, powerful tool is often not enough. Some information also comes from a network of weather watchers called Skywarn volunteers. They gather data about shifts in weather conditions in their neighborhoods and pass them on.

Predicting tornadoes is not an exact science. Fortunately, meteorologists are getting better at their job. As a result, more lives will be saved in the future.

PREWRITE

DRAFT

REVISE

PROOFREAD

PUBLISH

PRACTICE AND APPLY

Publish Your Own Report

1. Double-check your proofread draft.
2. Make a final copy of your report in your best handwriting or on a computer.
3. Add photos or diagrams to support your ideas and make your report more interesting.
4. Display your report on a weather bulletin board.

TECHNOLOGY

When you choose a typeface style for your report, remember that fancy or unusual typefaces are often difficult to read. Choose a plain, clear style that will not distract your readers.

Research Report

Score	Description
4 Excellent	■ creates an accurate, well researched, and detailed report ■ moves smoothly from a strong introduction to a final conclusion ■ has a fresh perspective and is involved in the topic ■ uses precise, colorful, and interesting language ■ includes a variety of sentences that flow smoothly ■ is free or almost free of errors
3 Good	■ creates a solid report with supporting details ■ has a clear introduction and conclusion with smooth transitions ■ uses an informed tone and some solid research ■ uses a variety of words appropriate to the topic ■ uses easy-to-follow sentences of different lengths ■ has minor errors that do not confuse the reader
2 Fair	■ creates a report but some facts are vague or not on topic ■ has problems with sequence and transitions ■ does not clearly connect with readers or show strong interest in the research ■ uses words mostly at or under grade level ■ includes mostly simple sentences ■ makes frequent errors that confuse the reader
1 Unsatisfactory	■ does not present a real report; writing has no focus ■ is structured poorly and is hard to follow ■ does not address readers and contains no research ■ relies on basic vocabulary and uses words vaguely or incorrectly ■ includes incomplete and confusing sentences ■ makes serious and repeated errors

Go to www.macmillanmh.com for a 6-Point Student Writing Rubric.

Unit 5

Expository Writing: Writing That Compares

Writing That Compares

Writing that compares often explains how two things are similar and how they are different. A comparison can help the reader understand an unfamiliar idea by relating it to a more familiar one. Writing that compares can also help the reader learn more about two familiar subjects.

Learning from Writers

Read the following examples of writing that compares. What information do the writers give you? As you read each example, look for clear similarities and differences between the subjects.

THINK AND WRITE

Purpose
How can comparisons help a writer explain ideas to the reader? Write a brief explanation in your journal.

Hurricane Rescue

What happened in Florida in 1992 is a good example of how pre-hurricane evacuations can save many lives. When Hurricane Andrew struck there, fewer than 40 people died. Of course, any loss of life in a hurricane is tragic, but compared with the 6,000 deaths that occurred during the Galveston, Texas, hurricane of 1900, the low number of deaths in Florida represents an incredible improvement.

More people died in the Galveston hurricane because in 1900 there were no weather satellites or computers to warn people about the storm. The deadliest hurricane on record, however, was in 1970 in Bangladesh, where some 500,000 people died. There were no advance warnings for that storm, too—by then, the technology was available, but Bangladesh was unable to afford such sophisticated equipment.

—Bill E. Neder, from *Hurricane Rescue*

Moving Legs Fast

Jogging and running seem the same, but they are different. Both are good ways to stay strong, healthy, and fit by moving the legs fast. Joggers do not compete with other people. They run to relax. By contrast, runners often race in competitions. They are concerned with speed and distance. Joggers take short steps and often land with their feet flat to the ground. Runners take longer steps and land on their toes. A jog is anything slower than six miles an hour. A run is anything faster than that pace. Although jogging and running are somewhat different, both provide good exercise.

–Raynell Johnson

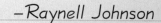

PRACTICE AND APPLY

Thinking Like a Reader

1. What is the main idea of "Hurricane Rescue"?

2. Name a main similarity and a main difference between running and jogging as described in "Moving Legs Fast."

Thinking Like a Writer

3. Why do you think the author of "Hurricane Rescue" chose to use comparisons to make his point?

4. How did the author of "Moving Legs Fast" organize his ideas to compare jogging and running?

5. **Reading Across Texts** Compare how the authors of "Hurricane Rescue" and "Moving Legs Fast" used comparison and contrast words to make their points.

Features of Writing That Compares

DEFINITIONS AND FEATURES

In writing that compares, the writer often explains how two things are alike or different. Writing that compares:

► Explains how two things are **similar**.

► Explains how two things are **different**.

► Organizes details in a **logical order**.

► Uses **comparison and contrast words** to make transitions from one idea to the next.

► Similarities

Reread "Hurricane Rescue" by Bill E. Neder on page 88. What are the similarities between the Galveston hurricane in 1900 and the hurricane in Bangladesh in 1970?

> More people died in the Galveston hurricane because in 1900 there were no weather satellites or computers to warn people about the storm. The deadliest hurricane on record, however, was in 1970 in Bangladesh . . . There were no advance warnings for that storm.

The author shows that there was no sophisticated equipment to protect either Galveston in 1900 or Bangladesh in 1970.

► Differences

Neder explains that pre-hurricane evacuations can save lives and made Hurricane Andrew different from the Galveston hurricane. What information does the author present to show this difference?

> When Hurricane Andrew struck there, fewer than 40 people died . . . compared with the 6,000 deaths that occurred during the Galveston, Texas, hurricane of 1900...

The author tells how many people died in each hurricane to make his comparison clear.

▶ Logical Order

There are two ways you can organize points in a comparison. You can discuss the features of one subject and then the features of your second subject. Or you can discuss one feature at a time, comparing and contrasting the two subjects on the basis of that feature.

> What happened in Florida in 1992 . . . More people died in the Galveston hurricane...The deadliest hurricane on record, however, was in 1970 in Bangladesh...

How did the author choose to organize his comparison?

▶ Comparison and Contrast Words

Comparison and contrast words lead the reader smoothly from idea to idea. Use comparison and contrast words, such as *both*, *too*, *similarly*, *also*, *on the one hand*, *on the other hand*, *however*, and *on the contrary*.

> Of course, any loss of life in a hurricane is tragic, but compared with the 6,000 deaths that occurred during the Galveston, Texas, hurricane of 1900...

Which comparison phrase did Neder use in "Hurricane Rescue"?

PRACTICE AND APPLY

Create a Venn Diagram

1. Make a diagram with two overlapping circles. Label the left-hand circle *Jogging*. Label the right-hand circle *Running*.
2. Reread "Moving Legs Fast" by Raynell Johnson on page 89.
3. List the differences in the parts of the circles that do not overlap. Write the similarities in the portion where the circles do overlap.
4. Below the diagram, list the comparison and contrast words Raynell used in his essay.

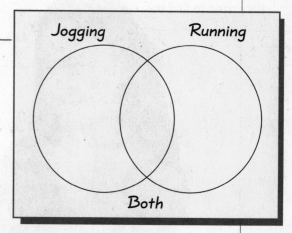

Prewrite

Writing that compares can inform readers about how two people, places, things, or ideas are alike and different. When you compare and contrast, you give your reader a clear understanding of how two items are like and unlike each other.

Purpose and Audience

Before writing, think about who will be reading your comparison. You can explain something unfamiliar to your reader by comparing it to something familiar. You can also contrast two subjects by pointing out their differences.

Writing that compares helps you organize ideas in a clear and logical way. How can you use comparisons to help your readers understand your ideas?

Choose a Topic

Start by **brainstorming** a list of topics you could compare. Think about your readers. What comparison would they find interesting? Then, choose one set of items you would like to compare.

Next, brainstorm traits the two items have in common. Then, think about how the two items are different. **Explore ideas** by making a list. Later, you will organize your ideas.

THiNK AND WRITE

Audience
Are your readers familiar with the subjects you are comparing? In your journal, list what you think they already know. Then list what they need to find out.

I got these ideas by brainstorming with my writing group.

Black Star, Bright Dawn by O'Dell
Iditarod Dream by Wood
Sled-dog races
Reasons to race
Courageous
Lead dog helps
Exciting
Illustrated? Photographs?
Fierce desire to win
Injured dogs?

Organize • Compare and Contrast

When writing to compare, think about similarities and differences. Then organize your ideas to make a clear, logical point. This writer left out some of her ideas and added others. How does the information she added make the comparisons clearer?

PREWRITE

DRAFT

REVISE

PROOFREAD

PUBLISH

SIMILARITIES AND DIFFERENCES CHART

Comparing Two Books:
Black Star, Bright Dawn and Iditarod Dream

Similarities	Differences
• Teenagers racing in Iditarod	• Bright Dawn, girl (O'Dell)
• Exciting	• Dusty, boy (Wood)
• Lead dogs help complete race	• long race (O'Dell)
• Courageous	• Jr. Iditarod (Wood)
• Fierce desire to win	• Bright Dawn races because of her father
	• Dusty wants to race

PRACTICE AND APPLY

Plan Your Own Writing That Compares

1. Consider your purpose and audience.
2. Brainstorm sets of items to compare.
3. Choose two items and chart similarities and differences.
4. Decide the main point you want to make to your audience.

Checklist ✓

Prewriting

- Did you think about your purpose and audience?

- Have you picked two items to compare?

- Did you make a list of traits for each item?

- How can you use a chart to organize your ideas?

- Do you need to do any research?

Prewrite • Research and Inquiry

▶ **Writer's Resources**

You may have to do research to get more information for your writing that compares. First, make a list of questions. Then decide what resources you need to answer your questions.

What Else Do I Need to Know?	Where Can I Find the Information?
How long is the Jr. Iditarod?	Use an electronic directory.
Which book is nonfiction?	Use parts of a book.

▶ **Use an Electronic Directory**

You can use an electronic directory, such as an Internet search engine, to find more information relating to your topic. Select a keyword to identify the topic you want to research. You may need to type in a more specific keyword or phrase if you don't find the information you need. Most librarians can help you use this resource.

Use the Help! section for instructions.

Type a keyword in the Search box.

Click the Search button to find articles about your keyword.

Click on an underlined word that may be related to your topic.

Go to other links on the Web.

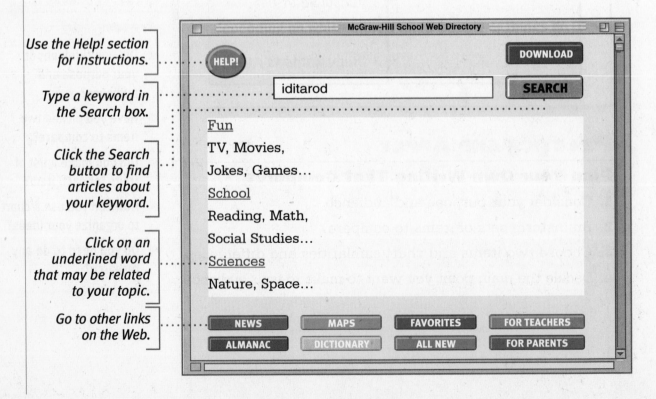

McGraw-Hill School Web Directory

HELP!   DOWNLOAD

iditarod   SEARCH

Fun
TV, Movies, Jokes, Games...
School
Reading, Math, Social Studies...
Sciences
Nature, Space...

NEWS   MAPS   FAVORITES   FOR TEACHERS
ALMANAC   DICTIONARY   ALL NEW   FOR PARENTS

▶ Use Parts of a Book

To find out if a book has the information you need for your topic, you can use different parts. The **Table of Contents** lists the title of each chapter or section. It tells you the page on which each one begins. The **Index** in a nonfiction book lists topics alphabetically with page numbers.

▶ Use Your Research

You can add the information gathered from your research to your comparison chart. This writer discovered new similarities and differences. How did she change her chart?

• Courageous

• Fierce desire to win

• long race (O'Dell)

• Jr. Iditarod (Wood)
  is 158 miles

• Bright Dawn races because of her father

• Dusty wants to race

• fiction (O'Dell)

• nonfiction (Wood)

PREWRITE

DRAFT

REVISE

PROOFREAD

PUBLISH

Checklist ✓

Research and Inquiry

■ Did you list questions about your topic?

■ Which resources might help answer these questions?

■ Did you take notes?

PRACTICE AND APPLY

Review Your Plan

1. Look back at your comparison chart.

2. List questions you have about your subject.

3. Identify the resources you will need to answer these questions.

4. Add new information to your chart.

Draft

Before you begin writing your draft, review your comparison chart. Think about organizing your paper. One way to organize is to move back and forth between two items, comparing and contrasting details of each. Another good way is to think about one subject at a time, listing descriptive details of one subject, then of the other. Sometimes details that are similar are stated first, followed by the traits that are different.

Main idea of first paragraph: Excitement of the Iditarod

SIMILARITIES AND DIFFERENCES CHART

Comparing Two Books:
Black Star, Bright Dawn and Iditarod Dream

Similarities	Differences
• Teenagers racing in Iditarod	• Bright Dawn, girl (O'Dell)
• Exciting	• Dusty, boy (Wood)
• Lead dogs help complete race	• long race (O'Dell)
• Courageous	• Jr. Iditarod (Wood) is 158 miles
• Fierce desire to win	• Bright Dawn races because of her father
	• Dusty wants to race
	• fiction (O'Dell)
	• nonfiction (Wood)

Main idea of second paragraph: Similarities

Main idea of third paragraph: Differences

✓ Checklist

Drafting

- Did you consider your purpose and audience?

- Have you stated your main idea clearly and supported it with details?

- Have you presented the most important similarities and differences of the two items you are comparing?

- Have you organized your ideas and supporting details in a clear, logical pattern?

Look at how the writer used the ideas in her comparison chart to write a first draft. She stated the main idea of her draft in the first paragraph. Then, in the following paragraphs, she pointed out the similarities and differences.

DRAFT

Black Star, Bright Dawn and Iditarod dream are similar. One book is fiction. The other is nonfiction. Each book describes the aventures of a teenager who participates in the Iditarod. Thanks to the authors, we can read an exciting book

> Main idea of draft

O'Dell's Bright Dawn, a girl and Woods Dusty, a boy both rely on the skill of their lead dog to complete the race. The characters have courage. They have a fierce desire to win.

> Supporting details show the similarities between the books.

There are key differences between the two books. Dusty races because he wants to. Bright Dawn runs because of her Father. Dusty joins the 158-mile Jr. Iditarod. Bright Dawn enters the longer race.

> Supporting details show the differences between the books.

No one who reads these books will ever forget the characters. No one who reads these books will ever forget the Iditarod.

> Conclusion

PRACTICE AND APPLY

Draft Your Own Writing That Compares

1. Review your comparison chart.
2. Decide on the main point you want to make.
3. Explain how the two items are similar.
4. Explain how the two items are different.
5. Organize supporting ideas clearly and logically.

TECHNOLOGY

Does your writing jump from one comparison to another? Rearrange the order by cutting and pasting text until your ideas flow smoothly and your meaning is clear.

Revise

Elaborate

One way to improve your writing is to elaborate. When you elaborate, you add important details that might be missing from your writing. When you revise, you may need to expand your details so they give more information or are more precise.

By adding details about the Iditarod, the writer gives more information about the subjects she is comparing.

> Each book describes the aventures of a teenager
> , Alaska's famous sled-dog race
> who participates in the Iditarod. ^

The writer explained Bright Dawn's motivation to show how she differs from Dusty.

> enters the race at the insistence   who cannot
>   compete
> Bright Dawn ~~runs because~~ of her Father.
>   ^   ^

Word Choice

When you are writing, it is important to use the right words to organize your ideas and communicate them clearly. Make sure you choose comparison and contrast words to make transitions from one idea to the next.

> Both
> The characters have courage. They have a fierce
>   ^   ^ also
> desire to win.
> However,
>   , There are key differences between the two books.
>   ^

COMPARE AND CONTRAST WORDS

both

too

similarly

also

in the same way

like

as

on the one hand

on the other hand

however

although

rather

instead

but

yet

whereas

on the contrary

otherwise

Better Sentences

As you continue to revise your draft, check your sentences for fluency and clarity. Read the sentences aloud. Do they flow well? Did you combine sentences to present information clearly?

Sometimes you can use compound subjects or objects to help your writing sound better. Because the subjects and predicates in the following sentences are the same, the objects can be combined.

PREWRITE

DRAFT

REVISE

PROOFREAD

PUBLISH

> No one who reads these books will ever forget the characters.
>
> No one who reads these books will ever forget the Iditarod.
>
> No one who reads these books will ever forget the characters or the Iditarod.

PRACTICE AND APPLY

Revise Your Own Writing That Compares

1. Add information to make similarities and differences clearer to your audience.

2. Use words that show comparisons and contrasts.

3. **Grammar** Combine sentences when possible by combining subjects or objects.

4. Use the correct forms of comparative and superlative adjectives to compare and contrast two or more persons, things, or ideas.

TECHNOLOGY

Review your text to see if any paragraphs need more details or examples. It is easy to add or delete information when working on a computer.

Revise • Peer Conferencing

Writing PROCESS

Now it is time to step back from your writing. Exchange drafts with a partner. Your partner may have fresh ideas that will help improve your writing.

Tell more about the books. Shouldn't you mention the authors?

Shouldn't the fiction/nonfiction difference be in a later paragraph?

Add more details to show the similarities and differences.

This conclusion repeats ideas.

Black Star, Bright Dawn and Iditarod dream are similar. One book is fiction. The other is nonfiction. Each book describes the aventures of a teenager who participates in the Iditarod. Thanks to the authors, we can read an exciting book

O'Dell's Bright Dawn, a girl and Woods Dusty, a boy both rely on the skill of their lead dog to complete the race. The characters have courage. They have a fierce desire to win.

There are key differences between the two books. Dusty races because he wants to. Bright Dawn runs because of her Father. Dusty joins the 158-mile Jr. Iditarod. Bright Dawn enters the longer race.

No one who reads these books will ever forget the characters. No one who reads these books will ever forget the Iditarod.

Conferencing for the Reader

■ Are features of writing that compares included in your partner's piece?

- similarities
- differences
- main idea with supporting details
- logical order
- comparing and contrasting words

■ Make sure to tell your partner what's good about the piece as well as what needs improvement.

When it is time to revise your writing that compares, think about the comments your partner made. This writer made some changes based on her partner's ideas.

REVISE

Scott O'Dell's   Ted Wood's
    Black Star, Bright Dawn and Iditarod dream are
        in some ways
similar. ~~One book is fiction. The other is nonfiction.~~

Each book describes the aventures of a teenager who
                    , Alaska's famous sled-dog race
participates in the Iditarod. Thanks to the authors, we

can read an exciting book

    O'Dell's Bright Dawn, a girl and Woods Dusty, a boy

both rely on the skill of their lead dog to complete the
        Both
race. ~~The~~ characters have courage. They have a fierce
                                    also

desire to win.
However,
    There are key differences between the two
O'Dell's book is fiction, whereas Wood's book is nonfiction.
    books. Dusty races because he wants to. Bright Dawn
enters
the race at the insistence   who cannot compete
~~runs because~~ of her Father. Dusty joins the 158-mile
                        traditional thousand-mile
Jr. Iditarod. Bright Dawn enters the ~~longer~~ race.

No one who reads these books will ever forget
        or the Iditarod
the characters. ~~No one who reads these books will~~

~~ever forget the Iditarod.~~

PRACTICE AND APPLY

Revise Your Own Writing That Compares

1. Use your conference notes to improve your writing.

2. Add details that will give your reader more information.

3. Use exact words to show similiarities and differences.

4. Choose words that make clear transitions between ideas.

Checklist ✓

Revising

- Does your writing suit your purpose and audience?

- Do any ideas need elaboration? Have you included enough details?

- Does your word choice clearly show similarities and differences?

- Are your ideas organized clearly?

- Do your sentences flow together well?

Proofread/Edit

After you have revised your draft, you will need to proofread and edit it to find and correct any mistakes in grammar, mechanics and usage, punctuation, and spelling.

STRATEGIES FOR PROOFREADING

- **Reread your revised paper several times.** Look for a different type of error each time. This will enable you to catch your mistakes.

- **Read each sentence for correct capitalization.** Every sentence begins with a capital letter. Remember that proper nouns must begin with capital letters, too.

- **Check for missing words.** Read each sentence to make sure you haven't omitted any words.

- **Check for spelling mistakes.** It helps if you start at the end of your paper and read backwards.

TECHNOLOGY

Use the spell checker on your computer, but don't forget to use your head, too. The computer can't tell whether the word you are checking is a plural noun, like *dogs*, or a possessive noun, like *dog's*, but you can.

REVIEW THE RULES

GRAMMAR

- **Adjectives** can be used to compare and contrast two or more people, places, things, or ideas. A **comparative adjective** is made by adding *-er* to most one-syllable (and sometimes two-syllable) adjectives. A **superlative adjective** compares more than two things. You usually form the superlative by adding *-est*.

- An **appositive** tells more about the noun it follows. Commas are used to set off most **appositives** from the rest of the sentence.

MECHANICS

- **Titles of books** are **underlined** and the first letter of each important word in the title should be **capitalized**.

Go to pages 138–173 to review other rules.

Look at the proofreading corrections made on the draft below. What does the symbol ≡ mean? Why does the writer want to change the lower case letter to a capital?

PROOFREAD

Scott O'Dell's   Ted Wood's
   Black Star, Bright Dawn and Iditarod dream are
   ^   ^   ≡
     in some ways

similar. ~~One book is fiction. The other is nonfiction.~~
             ^
                 (SP) adventures

Each book describes the ~~aventures~~ of a teenager who

          , Alaska's famous sled-dog race

participates in the Iditarod. Thanks to the authors, we
               ^

can read an exciting book⊙

    O'Dell's Bright Dawn, a girl‚ and Woods‚ Dusty, a boy‚

both rely on the skill of their lead dog to complete the
     Both
race. ~~The~~ characters have courage. They have a fierce
      ^   also

desire to win.
    However,
     There are key differences between the two
     ^
O'Dell's book is fiction, whereas Wood's book is nonfiction.
books. Dusty races because he wants to. Bright Dawn
enters
the race at the insistence   who cannot compete
~~runs because~~ of her Father‚ Dusty joins the 158-mile
                ^   traditional thousand-mile
Jr. Iditarod. Bright Dawn enters the ~~longer~~ race.
                   ^

No one who reads these books will ever forget
       or the Iditarod
the characters. ~~No one who reads these books will~~
           ^
~~ever forget the Iditarod.~~

PRACTICE AND APPLY

Proofread Your Writing That Compares

1. Capitalize all proper nouns.

2. Correct all spelling errors.

3. Use commas to set off appositives.

4. Use apostrophes correctly in possessive nouns.

Checklist ✓
Proofreading

- Did you correct capitalization errors?
- Did you spell every word correctly?
- Are the punctuation marks in the right places?
- Did you create compound sentences when possible?

PROOFREADING MARKS

#	new paragraph
^	add
℘	take out
≡	Make a capital letter.
/	Make a small letter.
(SP)	Check the spelling.
⊙	Add a period.

Publish

Writing
PROCESS

Before you publish, read your composition one more time to make sure you caught and corrected every error. Use a checklist to help you.

✓ **Self-Check** Writing That Compares

❑ Did I make my purpose clear? Did I stay on topic?

❑ Did I write in a way that will interest my readers and keep their attention?

❑ Did I compare important ideas? Did I use enough facts and details to make my point?

❑ Did I organize my writing logically?

❑ Did I use transition words to connect my ideas?

❑ Did I write a conclusion?

❑ Did I vary the length of my sentences, using simple and compound subjects and objects?

❑ Does my writing flow smoothly?

❑ Did I use comparative and superlative adjectives correctly?

This writer used the checklist to review her writing before making a final copy. Read "Adventures on Ice" and discuss it with a partner. Do you think she organized her writing well? Was it ready to be published?

Adventures on Ice
by Denise Maxwell

Scott O'Dell's <u>Black Star, Bright Dawn</u> and Ted Wood's <u>Iditarod Dream</u> are similar in some ways. Each book describes the adventures of a teenager who participates in the Iditarod, Alaska's famous sled-dog race. Thanks to the authors, we can read an exciting book.

O'Dell's Bright Dawn, a girl, and Wood's Dusty, a boy, both rely on the skill of their lead dog to complete the race. Both characters have courage. They also have a fierce desire to win.

However, there are key differences between the two books. O'Dell's book is fiction, whereas Wood's book is nonfiction. Dusty races because he wants to. Bright Dawn enters the race at the insistence of her father, who cannot compete. Dusty joins the 158-mile Jr. Iditarod. Bright Dawn enters the traditional thousand-mile race.

No one who reads these books will ever forget the characters or the Iditarod.

TECHNOLOGY

Experiment with different type styles for your final copy. Make sure the size and font are easy to read and suit your topic.

PRACTICE AND APPLY

Publish Your Own Writing That Compares

1. Check your revised draft one more time.

2. Make a neat, final copy of your draft.

3. Choose photographs, pictures, or maps that illustrate your similarities or differences.

Writing That Compares

Score	Description
4 Excellent	■ compares and contrasts two items or topics with supporting details ■ organizes the comparison logically with clear connections ■ uses a clear voice that shows detailed knowledge ■ uses details to create word pictures ■ writes a variety of sentences that flow smoothly ■ is free or almost free of errors
3 Good	■ compares and contrasts two items or topics ■ organizes the comparison logically with smooth connections ■ attempts to connect with readers in a voice that shows knowledge ■ uses a variety of adjectives ■ writes easy-to-follow sentences of varying lengths ■ has minor errors that do not confuse the reader
2 Fair	■ writes an unclear comparison with few details ■ does not organize the comparison logically or connect ideas ■ doesn't connect well with reader and shows incomplete knowledge ■ includes mostly ordinary language and errors in word usage ■ writes mostly simple, short sentences ■ makes frequent errors that confuse the reader
1 Unsatisfactory	■ does not write a focused comparison of two items or topics ■ has no organizational flow and lacks details ■ does not connect with readers ■ uses only general words or uses words incorrectly ■ includes incomplete and confusing sentences ■ makes serious and repeated errors

Go to www.macmillanmh.com for a 6-Point Student Writing Rubric.

Unit 6

Expository Writing: A How-To

Expository Writing: A How-to

How-to writing explains a process. This process may describe how to do something, how something works, or what causes an event to occur, for example.

Learning from Writers

Read the following examples of how-to writing. What are the writers explaining? Do you think their explanations are clear enough for readers to follow? As you read, think about how the writers chose to organize their ideas.

THINK AND WRITE

Purpose
Why do you think people write explanatory articles? Write your ideas in your journal.

EARTHQUAKES

There are forces inside the earth that bend and twist rock of the crust and upper mantle. They put the rock under great strain. When the strain becomes too great, the rock snaps.

You can see and feel the kind of thing that happens if you take a fairly thick stick and bend it. As you do, energy from your muscles is stored in the stick as strain. When you bend the stick past a certain point, it snaps, and the stored-up energy is suddenly released. The broken ends of the stick fly up, and you feel a sharp stinging in your hands. The stinging is something like the shaking caused by an earthquake.

—Patricia Lauber, from *Volcanoes and Earthquakes*

Making a Shadow Puppet

It's easy to make a shadow puppet. First, draw or trace a character and cut it out. Next, cut off the parts of the body that move, like legs, tail, and head.

Glue the body and its parts to cardboard for backing. Then cut out the pieces. Leave an inch of extra backing on the movable parts. When you put the parts together, the extra backing should overlap. Punch a hole through these overlapping pieces and attach these parts to the body with paper fasteners. Finally, attach wooden or wire rods to the body and to the movable parts. You use these rods to make the puppet move.

Now take a white cloth screen and put a light behind it. Move your puppet between the light and the screen. The puppet will make a shadow on the screen.

—Liz Choi

PRACTICE AND APPLY

Thinking Like a Reader

1. According to Patricia Lauber, what causes an earthquake to occur?

2. Name the main steps that you need to take to make a shadow puppet.

Thinking Like a Writer

3. In "Earthquakes," how does the author help the reader understand why earthquakes take place?

4. What spatial words does Liz Choi use to make her instructions easy to follow?

5. **Reading Across Texts** Compare the two literature models. Write about the author's purpose in each model.

Features of How-to Writing

DEFINITIONS AND FEATURES

In how-to writing, the writer describes a process step by step. Good how-to writing:

► **Informs** or **explains** how to complete a specific task or describes the cause of an effect.

► Presents a **logical series** of steps.

► Outlines **clear details** that are easy to follow.

► Uses **time-order** or **spatial words** to make steps clear.

► Informs or Explains

Reread "Earthquakes" on page 108. What process is the author explaining?

> When the strain becomes too great, the rock snaps.

The writer's first paragraph tells what causes an earthquake.

► A Series of Steps

A writer sometimes describes cause and effect relationships to explain steps in a process.

> When you bend a stick past a certain point, it snaps, and the stored-up energy is suddenly released.

What is the effect of bending the stick too far?

▶ Clear Details

Using clear details in how-to writing can make the process easier to understand.

> The broken ends of the stick fly up, and you feel a sharp stinging in your hands.

Why do you think these facts might capture the reader's attention? How do they help to explain what causes an earthquake?

▶ Spatial Words

In explaining how something works, it's important to tell how parts fit together. Use spatial words and phrases, such as *outside*, *above*, *near*, *over*, *next to*, and *on top of*.

> There are forces inside the earth that bend and twist rock of the crust and upper mantle.

What spatial word does the author use? How does this word help the reader understand what the writer is trying to explain?

PRACTICE AND APPLY

Create a Flow Chart

1. Reread "Making a Shadow Puppet" by Liz Choi on page 109.
2. List the steps needed to make a shadow puppet in a flow chart.
3. Draw the flow chart in the same sequence that the puppet would be built.
4. Write what you liked about Liz's how-to article.

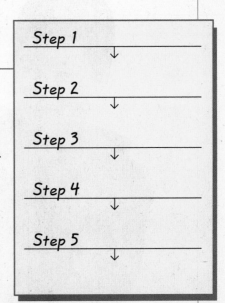

Step 1

Step 2

Step 3

Step 4

Step 5

Prewrite

How-to writing explains to the reader how to do something. In explanatory writing, you share information about a process that you know how to do.

Purpose and Audience

The purpose of how-to writing is to explain how to do something by describing a process, step by step.

Before writing, you need to think about your audience. Who will read your article? Will your readers need a clear explanation of every step?

Choose a Topic

Start by **brainstorming** a list of things you know how to do (or would like to learn how to do). Think about a topic that can be explained in a way that your readers will clearly understand.

After choosing your topic, **explore ideas** by making a list of the steps of the process. Later, you will put these steps in an order that makes sense. Also list details that you can add to make the process clear and interesting.

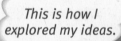

THINK AND WRITE

Audience
What age will most of the people in your audience be? Write about how the age level of your audience will affect the way you plan and write your how-to article.

This is how I explored my ideas.

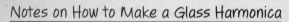

Notes on How to Make a Glass Harmonica

- Set the glasses in a row.
- Rub around the rim of each glass.
- Making a glass harmonica is easy and fun. Begin by filling eight glasses.
- Moisten index finger.
- Play a simple song.
- Experiment with the amount of water in each glass. The sound of the notes you play will change.

Organize • Sequence

If you explain the process of making something as a series of steps to follow, your readers will have an easier time understanding it. Note how this writer describes each step and the order in which the steps are presented.

PREWRITE

DRAFT

REVISE

PROOFREAD

PUBLISH

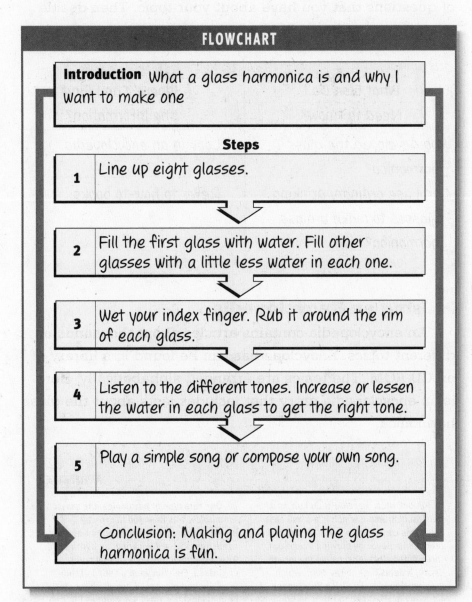

FLOWCHART

Introduction What a glass harmonica is and why I want to make one

Steps

1. Line up eight glasses.

2. Fill the first glass with water. Fill other glasses with a little less water in each one.

3. Wet your index finger. Rub it around the rim of each glass.

4. Listen to the different tones. Increase or lessen the water in each glass to get the right tone.

5. Play a simple song or compose your own song.

Conclusion: Making and playing the glass harmonica is fun.

Checklist ✓
Prewriting

■ Have you thought about your purpose and audience?

■ Have you chosen a topic and explored ideas about it?

■ Have you made a list of the steps in the process?

■ Have you checked the order of your steps?

■ Have you tried following the steps of your explanation?

■ Do you need to do any research?

PRACTICE AND APPLY

Plan Your Own Expository How-to Article

1. Think about your purpose and audience.

2. Brainstorm ideas for a topic. Choose your topic.

3. Think about the steps in the process.

4. Organize your steps in a flowchart.

Prewrite • Research and Inquiry

▶ Writer's Resources

It may be necessary to do research to get more information for your explanatory article. First, make a list of questions that you have about your topic. Then decide what resources you will need to answer your questions.

What Else Do I Need to Know?	Where Can I Find the Information?
Who developed the glass harmonica?	Look in an encyclopedia.
Can I use ordinary drinking glasses to make a glass harmonica?	Refer to how-to books.

▶ Using an Encyclopedia

An encyclopedia contains articles about thousands of different topics. Encyclopedias can be found in a library or on CD-ROM. The topics are arranged alphabetically. Here is an encyclopedia entry that includes facts about the glass harmonica.

The guide word at the top of a left-hand page shows the first entry on the page.

The entry word is followed by a respelling to help you pronounce the word.

The article contains facts about the entry word.

HARMONICA

HARMONICA, har MAHN uh kuh, is a musical instrument which is a small case with slots containing a series of metal reeds. It is played by blowing in and out through the slots. Also called the mouth organ, it dates back to the *aura*, which was developed by Friedrich Buschmann of Germany in 1821, and to the *symphonium*, which was created by Charles Wheatstone of England in 1829.

One rare type of harmonica, the *glass harmonica*, was invented in 1763 by Benjamin Franklin. The idea originally came from Richard Pockrich, an Irishman. After experimenting with several types of glasses, Franklin used a series of thin bowl-shaped glasses. When the finger was held against the glass's wet rim as the rim rotated, music resulted. This instrument was popular in the late 1700s.

Some words or names in the article may be separate entries in the encyclopedia.

▶ Using Other Sources

Various print resources, such as how-to manuals and guides, can be helpful sources of information. You can also use electronic resources to help you in your research. Look for CD-ROMs or informational videos that relate to your topic. You will find a list of the library's electronic reference materials at the reference desk.

▶ Putting It All Together

New information from your research can go into your flowchart. By using an encyclopedia, this writer learned who invented the glass harmonica. He also learned that different types of glasses produce different sounds. How did he add this information to his flowchart?

Introduction	What a glass harmonica is and why I want to make one. Benjamin Franklin invented it.

Steps

1	Line up eight glasses. must be thin; glasses with thick sides won't work well.

2	Fill the first glass with water. Fill other glasses with a little less water in each one.

Checklist ✓

Research and Inquiry

- ■ Did you list your questions?

- ■ Did you identify possible resources?

- ■ Did you take notes?

PRACTICE AND APPLY

Review Your Plan

1. Look at your sequence chart.

2. List questions you have about your topic.

3. Identify the resources you will need to find answers to your questions.

4. Add the new information to your chart.

Writing PROCESS

Draft

Before you begin writing your how-to article, review your sequence chart. Think about making a paragraph for every major step in the process. Also think about how the steps mentioned in your explanatory article need to be arranged so that the directions can be carried out.

> I'll make the first paragraph interesting by telling readers how Franklin invented the instrument.

> In the second paragraph, I need to make sure my readers understand how full the glasses should be.

FLOWCHART

Introduction What a glass harmonica is and why I want to make one. Benjamin Franklin invented it.

Steps

1. Line up eight glasses. must be thin; glasses with thick sides won't work well.

2. Fill the first glass with water. Fill other glasses with a little less water in each one.

3. Wet your index finger. Rub it around the rim of each glass.

4. Listen to the different tones. Increase or lessen the water in each glass to get the right tone.

5. Play a simple song or compose your own song.

Conclusion: Making and playing the glass harmonica is fun.

> The third paragraph, about playing the glass harmonica, could begin here.

✓ Checklist

Drafting

- Does your explanatory writing fit your purpose and your audience?

- Do your instructions include all the necessary steps?

- Are the steps in the correct order?

- Have you used words such as *inside, next to,* and *left* to make your instructions clear?

- After they read your explanatory article, will your readers be able to make a glass harmonica?

Look at how this student used the ideas in his chart to write a first draft. He used interesting facts to add an introduction to his explanatory article.

PREWRITE

DRAFT

REVISE

PROOFREAD

PUBLISH

DRAFT

Did you know that you can make music with glass and water. Benjamin Franklin. He figured out how to do it. he made something called the glass harmonica. All he did was moisten a finger and run it slowly around the rim of a goblet made of thin glass. A high-pitched sound was the result.

You can make your own glass harmonica. Gather eight thin glassses. Glasses with thick sides wont work well. Put the glassses in a row. Fill the glasses with water. Each glass should have less water.

Then, wet your index finger run it around the rims of the glasses. Each glass will have a different musical tone. Play a simple tune, such as "Twinkle, Twinkle, Little Star," or a tune you makes up. Experiment with various musical notes. Its fun!

The introductory paragraph gives the history of the glass harmonica.

Detailed instructions tell the reader how to arrange the glasses to make a glass harmonica.

This paragraph tells how to play the glass harmonica.

PRACTICE AND APPLY

Draft Your Own Expository How-to Article

1. Review your prewriting chart.
2. Put the steps of your explanation in order.
3. Use details to make the steps clear.

TECHNOLOGY

Try typing your notes into the computer before you begin your rough draft. With the Cut and Paste functions, it's easy to rearrange details to make sure you have them in the best order.

Revise

Elaborate

One way to improve your writing is to elaborate. When you elaborate in an explanatory article, you add important details and ideas that might be needed to clarify the steps of the process. For example, you might have to tell more about how something looks or sounds.

The writer added a detail to help the reader understand what a glass harmonica sounds like.

> that was almost like singing
> A high-pitched sound was the result.

To make the instructions clearer, the writer added the detail that the person playing the glass harmonica should start with the glass on the left.

> Then, wet your index finger run it around the
> , starting with the glass on the far left
> rims of the glasses.

Word Choice

When you are writing, it is important to choose just the right words for your topic and audience. In how-to writing, you need to choose spatial words that will help your reader visualize your instructions.

> than the one to the left of it
> Each glass should have less water.

SPATIAL WORDS

inside
outside
above
around
near
over
beside
right
left
closer
farther
up
down
on top of
next to
in the center of

Better Paragraphs

As you continue to revise your draft, look closely at each paragraph to make sure that all the sentences work well together to develop the main idea. If a sentence does not help to clarify the main idea, move it or delete it.

Sometimes you need to use transition or time-order words to connect ideas. Words such as *first, next, then,* or *finally* will help your sentences flow from one idea to the next.

PREWRITE

DRAFT

REVISE

PROOFREAD

PUBLISH

First,
︿Gather eight thin glassses. Glasses with thick
Then,   Next,
sides wont work well. Put the glassses in a row. Fill
︿   ︿

the glasses with water.

PRACTICE AND APPLY

Revise Your Own Expository How-to Article

1. Add details that will clarify your writing.

2. Use precise words to make your instructions easier to follow. Remember to use spatial words.

3. Take out unnecessary information.

4. **Grammar** Have you used the correct forms of modifying words and phrases?

TECHNOLOGY

You can use the cut-and-paste (or highlight-and-move) feature on your computer to change the order of paragraphs and sentences.

Revise • Peer Conferencing

Everyone could use a little help from a friend, so exchange drafts with a partner. He or she may have some helpful ideas or suggestions.

> Good first sentence. Second sentence is a fragment.

Did you know that you can make music with glass and water. Benjamin Franklin. He figured out how to do it. he made something called the glass harmonica. All he did was moisten a finger and run it slowly around the rim of a goblet made of thin glass. A high-pitched sound was the result.

You can make your own glass harmonica. Gather eight thin glassses. Glasses with thick sides wont work well. Put the glassses in a row. Fill the glasses with water. Each glass should have less water.

> You're missing information here.

Then, wet your index finger run it around the rims of the glasses. Each glass will have a different musical tone. Play a simple tune, such as "Twinkle, Twinkle, Little Star," or a tune you makes up. Experiment with various musical notes. Its fun!

> The steps in the process are not clear.

Conferencing for the Reader

■ Are features of expository how-to writing included in your partner's piece?
- explains how to complete a specific task
- presents step-by-step instructions
- outlines clear details that are easy to follow
- uses time-order or spatial words to make instructions clearer

■ Make sure to tell your partner what you like about the piece as well as what you think could be better.

As you revise your how-to article, think about the comments your partner made. This writer made some changes based on his partner's ideas.

REVISE

How To Make a Glass Harmonica

Did you know that you can make music with glass and water. Benjamin Franklin He figured out how to do it. he made something called the glass harmonica. All he did was moisten a finger and run it slowly around the rim of a goblet made of thin glass. A high-pitched sound ˄was the result. *that was almost like singing*

First,
You can make your own glass harmonica. ˄Gather eight thin glassses. Glasses with thick sides wont
Then,   *Next,*
work well. ˄Put the glassses in a row. ˄Fill the glasses
than the one to the left of it
with water. Each glass should have less water. ˄
and
Then, wet your index finger ˄run it around the
,starting with the glass on the far left
rims of the glasses. Each glass will have a different
Finally,
musical tone. ˄Play a simple tune, such as "Twinkle, Twinkle, Little Star," or a tune you makes up.
It's really interesting and entertaining!
Experiment with various musical notes. ~~Its fun!~~ ˄

PRACTICE AND APPLY

Revise Your Own Expository How-to Article

1. Read your draft aloud or listen as your partner reads it.

2. Jot down your partner's comments.

3. Make notes about what you want to change.

4. Add an appropriate title.

Checklist ✓
Revising

- Does your explanatory article suit your purpose and your audience?

- Do you need to elaborate on any part of your article?

- Did you present the steps in the right order?

- Do your sentences flow smoothly when read aloud?

- Did you use precise words? Did you include enough details?

- Did you use transition words to make your writing flow better? Did you use spatial words to make your writing easier to read?

Proofread/Edit

Writing PROCESS

After revising your explanatory article, proofread and edit it to find and correct any errors in mechanics, grammar and usage, and spelling.

STRATEGIES FOR PROOFREADING

- **Reread your revised paper several times.** Each time, look for a different type of error. You'll have a better chance of catching all the errors that way.

- **Read each sentence.** Check for correct capitalization and punctuation.

- **Reread for correct subject-verb agreement.** Make sure that each verb agrees with its subject.

- **Check for spelling mistakes.** Make sure you haven't mistaken words that sound alike, such as *its* and *it's*.

TECHNOLOGY

The spell checker on your computer can help you revise your work. However, a spell-check program is not foolproof. For example, it will not correct "wear" if you meant to type "where."

REVIEW THE RULES

GRAMMAR

- The subject and verb of a sentence must agree. Check their agreement by finding the simple subject and the simple predicate of each sentence.

MECHANICS

Remember these comma rules. Commas are used

- after each word in a series.

- to set off an appositive, an interrupter, or an introductory word.

Some verbs form a contraction with *not*. Example: *did not* becomes didn't. An apostrophe (') shows where a letter has been left out of a contraction.

Go to pages 138–173 to review other rules.

Look at the proofreading corrections made on the draft below. What does the symbol ∧ mean? When does the writer need to use that symbol?

PREWRITE

DRAFT

REVISE

PROOFREAD

PUBLISH

PROOFREAD

How To Make a Glass Harmonica

Did you know that you can make music with glass and water. Benjamin Franklin. He figured out how to do it. he made something called the glass harmonica. All he did was moisten a finger and run it slowly around the rim of a goblet made of thin glass. A high-pitched sound was the result. that was almost like singing

You can make your own glass harmonica. First, Gather eight thin glassses. Glasses with thick sides won't work well. Then, Put the glassses in a row. Next, Fill the glasses with water. Each glass should have less water. than the one to the left of it

Then, wet your index finger and run it around the rims of the glasses. starting with the glass on the far left Each glass will have a different musical tone. Finally, Play a simple tune, such as "Twinkle, Twinkle, Little Star," or a tune you makes up. It's really interesting and entertaining! Experiment with various musical notes. Its fun!

Checklist ✓
Proofreading

- Did you use commas where needed?
- Did you spell all the words correctly?
- Did you make sure subjects and verbs agree?
- Did you make sure verb tenses are correct?
- Did you end each sentence with the correct punctuation?
- Did you add a good title?

PROOFREADING MARKS

¶ new paragraph

∧ add

ℐ take out

≡ Make a capital letter.

/ Make a small letter.

ⓈⓅ Check the spelling.

⊙ Add a period.

PRACTICE AND APPLY

Proofread Your Own Expository How-to Article

1. Insert commas and apostrophes where needed.
2. Correct spelling errors.
3. Correct subject-verb agreement errors.
4. Capitalize words correctly.

Publish

Before you publish your writing, take a few minutes to review it one last time. The checklist below can help you.

✓ Self-Check How-to Writing

- ❑ Who was my audience? Did I write in a way that will interest them?
- ❑ Did I clearly present step-by-step instructions?
- ❑ Did I provide clear details that are easy to follow?
- ❑ Did I check for subject-verb agreement?
- ❑ Did I use modifying words and phrases properly?
- ❑ Did I use transition words?
- ❑ Did I use spatial words to make the instructions clearer?
- ❑ Were my sentences varied? Did they fit together well?
- ❑ Did I proofread and correct all errors?

The writer used the checklist for one more review of his explanatory article. Read the writer's published piece, "How to Make a Glass Harmonica," and discuss it with a small group. Do you think you could follow the directions to make a glass harmonica? Why or why not?

How to Make a Glass Harmonica
by Daniel D. Sohn

Did you know that you can make music with glass and water? Benjamin Franklin figured out how to do it. He made something called the glass harmonica. All he did was moisten a finger and run it slowly around the rim of a goblet made of thin glass. A high-pitched sound that was almost like singing was the result.

You can make your own glass harmonica. First, gather eight thin glasses. Glasses with thick sides won't work well. Then, put the glasses in a row. Next, fill the glasses with water. Each glass should have less water than the one to the left of it.

Then, wet your index finger and run it around the rims of the glasses, starting with the glass on the far left. Each glass will have a different musical tone. Finally, play a simple tune, such as "Twinkle, Twinkle, Little Star," or a tune you make up. Experiment with various musical notes. It's really interesting and entertaining!

Handwriting

If you're not using a computer to type your article, use your best handwriting to make a neat, final copy. Your piece will look neater if all of the lower parts of letters like *j, g, p,* and *y* are the same length.

PRACTICE AND APPLY

Publish Your Own Explanatory Writing

1. Check your revised draft one more time.

2. Make a neat, final copy.

3. Add a border, pictures, a cover, or all three.

How-to Writing

Score	Description
4 Excellent	■ creates a focused, interesting explanation with clear details ■ presents steps in a logical order using time-order words ■ speaks directly to reader ■ uses precise words that help understanding ■ uses a variety of simple and complex sentences ■ is free or almost free of errors
3 Good	■ creates a clear explanation ■ presents steps in a logical order ■ makes an effort to speak to readers ■ uses a variety of appropriate words ■ includes a variety of easy-to-follow sentences ■ has minor errors that do not confuse the reader
2 Fair	■ attempts an explanation, but some points are unclear ■ does not present information in a step-by-step order ■ does not connect to readers ■ uses vague words ■ writes mostly simple, short sentences ■ makes frequent errors that confuse the reader
1 Unsatisfactory	■ does not present an explanation ■ does not present information in a step-by-step order ■ does not make a connection with the reader ■ uses words that are inappropriate ■ includes incomplete and choppy sentences ■ makes serious and repeated errors

Go to www.macmillanmh.com for a 6-Point Student Writing Rubric.

Main Idea

A writer usually states the main idea of a paragraph in a topic sentence. The rest of the sentences in the paragraph provide details that support the main idea.

GUIDELINES

- The main idea is the most important thought in a piece of writing. The main idea is usually stated in a topic sentence.

- In a paragraph, all the sentences should work together to support one main idea.

- Supporting details develop the main idea by providing explanation and giving examples, facts, or opinions.

- The main idea and supporting details should be placed in a logical order.

- Use time-order words, such as *first*, *then*, and *after*, to connect ideas.

THINK AND WRITE

Main Idea
How does your writing become focused when you decide on a main idea? Write a brief explanation in your journal.

Read this paragraph about a personal experience. Notice how the writer states the main idea and uses supporting details to develop that idea.

The topic sentence states the main idea of the paragraph.

Time-order words make the sequence of events clear.

Supporting details help to develop or clarify the main idea.

I found the best dog of all time at an animal shelter. For a long time, I had been asking my parents if we could get a puppy. One day, we all went to the animal shelter. We saw great puppies of all shapes and sizes. I heard barking coming from behind me. There stood a puppy with huge brown eyes. As soon as I saw this frisky mutt, I knew we would become best friends.

Outlining

A writer uses an outline to organize related ideas before beginning to write. Making an outline will help you create a well-organized piece of writing containing main topics, subtopics, and details.

GUIDELINES

- Use an outline to help you plan your writing.

- The title of the outline states the topic.

- Outlines consist of main ideas indicated by Roman numerals.

- List subtopics beneath each main idea. These subtopics should support the main idea and should be indicated by capital letters.

- Give supporting details under each subtopic, indicated by numbers.

- Place the ideas in the outline in a logical order.

THINK AND WRITE

Outlining
Why do writers outline ideas before writing? Think about how outlining can improve the final written work. Write your answer in your journal.

Look at the following outline. Notice the placement of Roman numerals, capital letters, and numbers.

School Fall Festival

I. Festival Events

  A. Arts and Crafts

    1. From Various Cultures

    2. Recycled Materials

  B. Carnival Rides

  C. Games

    1. Team Sports

    2. Ring Toss

II. Where Money Will Go

  A. Library

    1. New Books

    2. Computer

  B. Playground

    1. Paint

    2. Benches

The title tells the main idea of the outline.

Main ideas are marked with Roman numerals.

Subtopics relate to main idea marked with the Roman numeral. Notice the capital letters used to indicate subtopics.

Details support the subtopics and are indicated by numbers.

Organization

A writer can choose from a number of methods when organizing a written piece. Whichever the writer chooses, the goal is to make the writing more understandable for the reader.

GUIDELINES

- **Spatial descriptions** describe how things are arranged. For example, spatial descriptions could use words such as *left*, *right*, *above*, *near*, *in front of*, or *outside*.

- To help set up an organized sequence of steps, use time-order words such as *first*, *next*, *then*, *before*, and *after*.

- When events occur because of the effect of some action, then use cause-and-effect words, such as *caused* and *because*.

THINK AND WRITE

Organization

Why is it important for explanatory writing to be organized in a logical way? Write a brief response in your journal.

Read this paragraph about how to make a fruit drink. Notice how the writer organizes the steps. Look for spatial, time-order, and cause-and-effect words.

The time-order words in the second and third sentences clarify what order to follow.

Spatial words help clarify location.

Placing the liquids in the blender first will cause the blender to work better.

It's fun to make a delicious "smoothie." First, get out an electric blender, and get an adult to help you use it. Then gather your ingredients. Arrange them next to the blender. My favorites are these: one cup of orange juice, one scoop of frozen yogurt, a banana, and four or five strawberries. Put them into the blender in that order, because the blender works better when liquid ingredients are at the bottom. Firmly put the blender's lid in place and turn on the blender. When your smoothie is well mixed, pour it into a glass and enjoy it.

Writing Descriptions

Writing a description is like painting a picture with words. You can use vivid descriptions to help your audience see what you see, hear what you hear, and feel what you feel.

GUIDELINES

- **Descriptions** are vivid word pictures of a person, place, or thing.

- **Descriptions can present broad views or close-ups.**

- **Sensory details that appeal to sight, sound, taste, touch, and smell can add richness to descriptions of everyday things.**

- **The order of details in a description should be presented in an order that makes sense, such as spatial order, front-to-back, or left-to-right.**

Read this descriptive paragraph. Notice how the writer presents a broad view, includes sensory details, and arranges details in a sensible order.

THiNK AND WRITE

Description
Why is description an important part of almost every type of writing? Write a brief explanation in your journal.

> Far, far north on Earth, a small band of men struggled against icy blasts of wind. The howling Arctic gales drove needles of ice into their faces. The bitter east wind was like a sharp sword, slicing right through the thick fur parkas. It was 60 degrees below zero, so cold that the men's noses, cheeks, and toes turned black with frostbite. But Robert Peary and Matthew Henson were determined to be the first men to reach the North Pole—or die trying.

The broad view of the Arctic is that of a harsh, extremely cold place.

Details appeal to touch, sight, and sound.

Details are arranged in spatial order.

Writing Dialogue

Using dialogue in writing is an effective way of enabling the reader to get to know the character. What the character says and how it is said portrays her or his personality. Dialogue also helps to hold the reader's attention.

THINK AND WRITE

Writing Dialogue

Why would you include dialogue in a story that you write? Respond in your journal.

GUIDELINES

- **Dialogue** is the exact words that characters speak in a story.

- Use **quotation marks** around a **quotation**, a speaker's exact words.

- Begin the first word of a quotation with a **capital letter**.

- Begin a **new paragraph** each time the speaker changes.

- Use **dialogue words**, such as *said* or *shouted*, to show who is speaking and to express the emotion of the characters.

- Use a **comma** to separate dialogue words from the quotation.

Read this short story. Notice how the writer used dialogue within the story.

By using dialogue, the writer brings the character and the setting to life.

Starting a new paragraph when the speaker changes makes the dialogue easier to follow.

The writer identifies the speaker by using the dialogue word said.

Several friends went canoeing down a calm, winding river on a crisp fall day. "What a beautiful sight!" exclaimed Francine as she looked at the trees changing color. "What do you think, Ramon?"

Ramon replied, "I have never seen so many wonderful colors. I'm glad we chose to go canoeing today."

"It is so peaceful," said Emily, "to watch the leaves glide down to the water and float downstream." The friends silently paddled the canoes further down the river. Everyone enjoyed the serene beauty and relaxing canoe trip.

Leads and Endings

In persuasive writing, a writer begins with a strong lead that grabs the audience's attention and concludes with a convincing ending.

GUIDELINES

- A lead is the first part of a piece of writing.

- Write a strong lead to grab the reader's attention.

- You may state your main idea or opinion in the lead.

- An ending is the last part of a piece of writing.

- Write a good ending to give your reader a feeling of closure, or completeness.

- Use the ending to state the strongest argument, draw a conclusion, summarize, or restate the main idea.

Read this persuasive piece from a student newspaper. Notice how the writer begins and ends the paragraph.

THINK AND WRITE

Leads and Endings

Why do you think a strong lead such as a question, snappy dialogue, or a powerful statement can help grab the reader's attention?

Would you like to enrich your life and gain great personal rewards? Then join the Outdoors Express! The Outdoors Express is comprised of a group of enthusiastic, committed, and fun-loving students who are devoted to caring for the earth. Past projects have included seeding prairie grasses around the school and recycling clothing and school supplies by donating them to needy communities. All members of the Outdoors Express agree that it brings them great fulfillment.

A strong lead grabs the reader's attention.

A good ending stresses the writer's strongest argument.

Writing

Book Review

A **book review** does two things. It tells what a book is about and gives you, the reviewer, an opportunity to tell your opinion of the book.

Write the title of the book and the author's name.

The Phantom Tollbooth by Norton Juster

Always begin with a strong introduction to grab your audience's attention.

Ten-year-old Milo is bored. He is convinced that everything is a waste of time. But one day, a tollbooth suddenly appears in his bedroom. Because he has nothing else to do, Milo decides to jump in his toy car and go through the mysterious tollbooth. The story develops around a mission that is assigned to Milo in The Lands Beyond. He must find and return two princesses.

The body should give the setting, or when and where the story takes place, as well as the characters, and one or two events from the plot.

Is the book funny, happy, scary, exciting, or sad?

This is a fascinating story of excitement and mystery. If you enjoy magical adventures with a lot of unexpected twists and turns, you will love this book just as much as I did.

The conclusion should contain your opinion of the book. Did you like it? Would you recommend it to others?

Practice Select a book you have recently read. Fold a piece of paper in half so that it opens like a book. Draw a scene from the book on the front of the folded paper. Write a book review inside. Then exchange book reviews with a classmate, and decide whether you would like to read each other's books.

Research Report

A **research report** contains facts and information about a particular topic. Research reports are written to explain.

Writing

The Amazon River

The Amazon River is the greatest river in South America. Beginning high in the Andes Mountains of Peru, the Amazon and its tributaries flow 4,000 miles to the Atlantic Ocean. The Amazon is also the world's largest river in water volume and in the area of its drainage basin. In fact, it drains 2,722,000 square miles (7,050,000 square kilometers)!

Often the subject of legends, the enormous Amazon has played an important role in the history of civilization.

Choose a title for your report that relates to your topic.

Write a main-idea sentence for each paragraph.

Use facts and supporting details to write sentences that explain each main idea.

Connect your points by using transition words.

Write a conclusion that summarizes the facts and information you have presented.

GUIDELINES

- Think of a topic that you would like to research.
- Consider your purpose and your audience.
- Investigate facts and information using a variety of sources.
- On index cards, take notes on the main ideas and important facts.
- Make an outline based on your notes.
- List your sources at the end of your report.

Practice Choose a topic for a research report. Use at least two sources. Take clear notes and use them to write an outline. Write a report based on your outline.

135

Writing

Humorous Play

A **humorous play** tells a funny story through the use of dialogue, characters, stage directions, and scenery. A play is usually performed in front of an audience.

Base your title on the plot.

Name and briefly describe your **characters**.

Describe the **setting**, when and where the story takes place.

Suggest **props** and **costumes**.

Use stage directions to tell the characters when and how to move on stage.

Include **dialogue**, or spoken parts, for each character.

The Price of a Smell

Characters:
 JUDGE: A wise old woman
 VINCE: A poor young painter
 CHEF LEGREED: A greedy man

Setting: A courtroom

Props: five silver dollars

Costumes: black robe for judge

As the play opens, a judge is sitting behind a desk. Chef LeGreed and Vince are standing in front of her.

VINCE: Your Honor, this man is trying to steal from me.

CHEF LEGREED: That's a lie. I only want what is due me.

JUDGE: Quiet! One at a time. *(Speaking to LeGreed)* You first.

CHEF LEGREED: This Vince rents a room above my restaurant. I heard him tell a friend that he was stealing from me.

VINCE: Smells, Your Honor. All I take is the smell of the food coming up from the restaurant.

JUDGE: *(Looking at Vince)* What do you do with the smells?

VINCE: The only food I can afford is noodles. The smells from the restaurant help me imagine that I'm eating a fine dinner.

JUDGE: *(To Chef LeGreed)* And how much do you want to be paid for these smells, sir?

CHEF LEGREED: I want the five silver dollars he always carries.

VINCE: But my mother gave me those to save for an emergency.

JUDGE: *(To Vince)* Drop the coins onto the table one at a time. *(Vince drops the coins.)* Case dismissed.

CHEF LEGREED: What do you mean? I didn't get paid.

JUDGE: You were concerned about SMELLS being stolen. Vince has now repaid you in SOUNDS—the sounds of the coins dropping.

Practice Write a short play based on a joke or funny story. Include setting, plot, characters, dialogue, and stage directions. Perform the play for the class.

Poem

A **poem** is an expressive form of writing that allows you to describe, persuade, explain, or tell a story. Poems use word pictures, special forms, sounds, rhyme, and rhythm to communicate thoughts and feelings.

The Road Not Taken

Two roads diverged in a yellow wood,
And sorry I could not travel both
And be one traveler, long I stood
And looked down one as far as I could
To where it bent in the undergrowth;

Then took the other, just as fair,
And having perhaps the better claim,
Because it was grassy and wanted wear;
Though as for that the passing there
Had worn them really about the same,

And both that morning equally lay
In leaves no step had trodden black.
Oh, I kept the first for another day!
Yet knowing how way leads on to way,
I doubted if I should ever come back.

I shall be telling this with a sigh
Somewhere ages and ages hence:
Two roads diverged in a wood, and I—
I took the one less traveled by,
And that has made all the difference.

—*by Robert Frost*

Choose an appropriate *title* for your poem. Capitalize the first letter of each important word in the title.

This poet used *rhyming words* to create interesting sounds in his poem.

This poem is divided into *stanzas,* or groups of lines that rhyme. You can use this *form,* or another one for your poem.

Use *sensory words* to make descriptions more vivid.

Practice Think about the world around you. Do you see anything that inspires you? Let your imagination guide you as you write your own poem.

Grammar

RULE 1

Sentences and Sentence Fragments

- A **sentence** is a group of words that expresses a complete thought.

  The trees are changing color.

- A **sentence fragment** is a group of words that does not express a complete thought.

  are changing (missing a subject) *The trees* (missing a predicate)

Practice: Rewrite each pair of sentence fragments as a complete sentence.

1. The temperature. Is starting to drop outside.

2. Days. Are getting shorter.

3. The sun. Sets earlier and earlier every night.

RULE 2

Kinds of Sentences

- There are four different types of sentences.

Sentence Types	Examples
A **declarative sentence** makes a statement.	*Our teacher planned a field trip.*
An **interrogative sentence** asks a question.	*Are parents going?*
An **imperative sentence** gives a command or makes a request.	*Please let us buy our lunch.*
An **exclamatory sentence** expresses strong feeling.	*Wow, they have a real spacesuit!*

Practice: Write each sentence. Place the correct punctuation mark at the end and write what type of sentence it is.

1. Our field trip is next Wednesday

2. Wow, you're in my group

3. Let's look at the exhibits now

4. When should we meet back at the bus

5. What a great field trip it was

RULE 3

Combining Sentences: Compound Sentences

- A compound sentence is a sentence that contains two sentences joined by a comma and a conjunction such as *and*, *but*, or *or*.

  The fire alarm went off, and it woke us up.

Practice: Rewrite each pair of simple sentences using a comma and the conjunction *and, but*, or *or*.

1. I saw a yellow blaze. I was frozen still.

2. Should I see if anyone is in the house? Should I call 911?

3. I ran to my neighbor's house. I used the phone.

RULE 4

Combining Sentences: Complex Sentences

- A complex sentence contains an independent clause and one or more dependent clauses.

  We got very wet while we were boating.

- An independent clause can stand alone as a sentence.

  We got very wet.

- A dependent clause cannot stand alone as a sentence and begins with a conjunction.

  While we were boating

- Use a comma after the dependent clause when it comes at the beginning of a sentence.

Practice: Combine the clauses to form complex sentences. Write the sentences, underlining the conjunctions.

1. We decided to go boating. Because it was a beautiful day.

2. If we had known how windy it would be. We would have waited.

3. Because of our experiences that day. I am taking lessons in boating.

 QUICK WRITE Write five complex sentences. Circle the conjunctions in red.

Grammar

RULE 5 — Complete Subjects and Complete Predicates

- A complete subject includes all the words in a sentence that tell whom or what the sentence is about.

   *The horse **ran very fast**.*

- The complete predicate includes all the words in a sentence that tell what the subject does or is.

   *The horse **ran very fast**.*

- A complete sentence must have both a complete subject and a complete predicate.

Practice: Write each sentence. Then draw a line between the complete subject and the complete predicate.

1. The horse was brown and white.
2. A pony ride was going to cost five dollars.
3. We waited in line for half an hour.

RULE 6 — Simple Subjects and Simple Predicates

- The simple subject is the main word or words in the complete subject.

   The horse galloped wildly in the field.

- The simple predicate is the main word or words in the complete predicate. It is always a verb.

   The horse galloped wildly in the field.

Practice: Write each sentence. Then draw one line under the simple subject and two lines under the simple predicate.

1. I rode the brown horse.
2. Several ponies trotted in a circle.
3. One horse swatted a fly with its tail.
4. We practiced for the horse show.
5. I hoped to win a blue ribbon.

RULE 7

Combining Sentences: Compound Subjects

- A **compound subject** has two or more simple subjects with the same predicate. Use the word *and* or *or* to join the parts of the compound subject.

  I rode in an airplane. My dad rode in an airplane.

  My dad and I rode in an airplane.

Practice: Write each pair of sentences as one sentence, making a compound subject.

1. Dad climbed aboard the plane. I climbed aboard the plane.

2. Mia waved at the plane. Kevin waved at the plane.

3. The passengers thanked the pilot. The crew thanked the pilot.

RULE 8

Combining Sentences: Compound Predicates

- A **compound predicate** has two or more simple predicates with the same subject. Use the word *and*, *or*, or *but* to join the parts of a compound predicate.

  Christie made a snowball. Christie threw a snowball.

  Christie made and threw a snowball.

Practice: Combine each pair of sentences by making a compound predicate. Write the new sentence.

1. My class will earn an extra recess. My class will lose an extra recess.

2. We will play after school. We will study after school.

3. Kristen dances under the tree. Kristen sings under the tree.

 QUICK WRITE Write five compound subjects and compound predicates. Underline the words you choose to connect the subjects and predicates.

Grammar

Grammar

RULE 1

Nouns

- A **noun** names a person, place, thing, or idea. It can be a single word or a group of words used together.

Person	Place	Thing	Idea
boy	store	book	sadness

Practice: Write each sentence. Circle the noun. Write whether the noun names a person, place, thing, or idea.

1. The kids in my class want to do a special project.
2. The class decided to make a mural for the front entrance.
3. My teacher distributed paper, paint, and markers.

RULE 2

Singular and Plural Nouns

- A **singular noun** names one person, place, thing, or idea.

  The cookie was freshly baked.

- A **plural noun** names more than one person, place, thing, or idea.

  The kids were excited to have a treat.

Practice: Write each sentence. Replace the word in parentheses ( ) with the plural form of that word.

1. Our neighbor gave us two (ticket) to the hockey game.
2. Before I could go, I had some (responsibility) to take care of at home.
3. As soon as I finished, I put on one of my favorite (jersey).
4. I went straight to the game and met some of my (friend).
5. We watched a player make two (goal) in the first period.

RULE 3

More Plural Nouns

- Add *-s* to form the plural of most nouns ending in *f* or *fe*. Some words ending in *f* or *fe* require you to change the *f* to *v* and add *-es*.

  chef—chefs   *knife—knives*

- To form the plural of nouns ending in a vowel and *o*, add *-s*. To form the plural of nouns that end with a consonant and *o*, add *-s* or *-es*.

  studio—studios   *piano—pianos*

- Some irregular nouns have special plural forms. Some irregular nouns have the same singular and plural forms.

  child—children   *moose—moose*

Practice: **Write each sentence. Write the plural form of the word in parentheses ( ).**

1. Last year I wrote a story about a family of (moose).

2. This year my story focused on a group of (deer).

3. Next year I will write about some (wolf) that live in the forest.

 RULE 4

Common and Proper Nouns

- A common noun names any person, place, thing, or idea.

  lady   *restaurant*   *book*

- A proper noun names a specific person, place, thing, or idea. It is always capitalized.

  Mrs. Escobar   *Texas*   *Statue of Liberty*

Practice: **Rewrite each sentence. Use capital letters for the proper nouns. Circle each common noun.**

1. The meteorologist predicted the hurricane in florida.

2. Newscasters announced that north carolina was hit.

3. hurricane floyd kept everyone in the house for three days.

 QUICK WRITE Brainstorm a list of five common nouns and five proper nouns in your home.

Grammar

RULE 5

Possessive Nouns

- A **possessive noun** names who or what has or owns something.

- Form a **singular possessive noun** by adding an **apostrophe** and *s* (*'s*).

  boy—boy's

- Form a **plural possessive noun** of a noun ending in *s* by adding an apostrophe (*'*) to the end of the word.

  girls—girls'

- Form a **plural possessive noun** of a plural noun not ending in *s* by adding an **apostrophe** and *s* (*'s*).

  men—men's

Practice: Write each phrase using the possessive form.

1. the hats of the ladies
2. the collar of the jacket
3. the rules of the contest
4. the car of Ms. Ying
5. the floors of the tents

RULE 6

Appositives

- An **appositive** is a word or group of words that follows a noun. It identifies or tells more about the noun it follows. **Commas** are used to set off most appositives from the rest of the sentence.

  Bill, my skiing partner, wore his new coat.

- Use an **appositive** to combine two short sentences into one.

  Evergreen has steep slopes. Evergreen is where we usually ski.

  Evergreen, where we usually ski, has steep slopes.

Practice: Write a new sentence by using an appositive to combine the two sentences in each pair.

1. Nick came with us on our ski trip. Nick is my best friend.
2. Sari led us up the mountain. Sari is our instructor.
3. The chair lift moved fast. A chair lift is a device that takes people up the mountain.

Grammar

RULE 7

Combining Sentences: Nouns

- If two sentences have the same predicate but different subjects, you can join the subjects with the connecting word *and* or *or* to make a **compound subject**.

  Shana fed the baby. Terrence fed the baby.

  Shana and Terrence fed the baby.

- If two sentences have the same subject but different objects, you can join the objects with the connecting word *and* or *or*.

  The baby ate peaches. The baby ate yogurt.

  The baby ate peaches or yogurt.

Practice: Write a sentence with a compound subject or object using the sentence given and one of your own. Write *CS* if your sentence has a compound subject, and *CO* if it contains a compound object.

1. Molly will baby-sit.

2. The baby likes to pull hair.

3. Feeding time is important.

4. Peas are a favorite food.

5. Maurice signed up for an infant-care class.

RULE 1

Action Verbs

- An **action verb** is a word that expresses action. It tells what the subject of the sentence does or did.

  The child dropped the ball.

Practice: Write each sentence. Complete the sentence with an action verb.

1. Many birds _____ in the nature preserve.

2. They _____ for food within the boundaries of the preserve.

3. They _____ their nests and _____ their young on the preserve.

 QUICK WRITE Write five sentences with compound subjects. Underline the subjects in each sentence.

Grammar

Direct and Indirect Objects

- A **direct object** is a noun or pronoun in the predicate that receives the action of a verb. It answers the question *what?* or *whom?* after an action verb.

    Sarah used her computer. (What did Sarah use? Her computer.)

- An **indirect object** usually comes before the direct object. It answers the question *to what? for what? to whom?* or *for whom?* after an action verb.

    Sarah gave her mom a card. Sarah gave a card to her mom.

Practice: **Write each sentence. Circle the verb. Write *DO* above the direct object and *IO* above the indirect object.**

1. I throw crumbs to the pigeons.
2. I gave my sister some crumbs, too.
3. The man told us facts about homing pigeons.

Verb Tenses

- The **tense** of a verb tells when an action takes place. Verbs not only express actions; they also tell when these actions take place.

Verb Tenses	Meaning	Examples
present	something that is happening now	*Janice discovers something new in her garden every day.*
past	something that has already happened	*She dug the garden last spring.*
future	something that will happen in the future	*She will plant eggplant next year.*

Practice: **Write the verb in each sentence. Then write whether it is in the present, past, or future tense.**

1. I watched some cartoons yesterday.
2. That outrageous character is so funny!
3. I will go to art school after high school.

146

RULE 4 — Subject-Verb Agreement

- A verb must agree with its subject. Add *-s* to most verbs if the subject is singular. Do not add *-s* if the subject is plural or *I* or *you*.

  Kristene parks her car on the street.

  Marla and Osvaldo park their car in a garage.

- When parts of a compound subject are joined by *or, either...or*, or *neither...nor*, the verb agrees with the subject that is nearer to it.

  Neither Kristen nor her cousins live in the suburbs.

Practice: Write each sentence, making plural subjects singular. Change each verb so that it agrees.

1. The children enjoy Ireland.

2. Their grandparents live there.

3. Every summer the women visit for four weeks.

RULE 5 — Main Verbs and Helping Verbs

- A verb phrase is a verb that contains more than one word. The last word is the main verb. All other words are helping verbs. A helping verb helps the main verb show an action or make a statement.

  We have been making some strides in that direction.

Common Helping Verbs

am, are, is; do, does, did; will, would; was, were; be, being, been;
shall, should; have, has, had; may, might, must; can, could

Practice: Write each verb phrase. Underline the main verb.

1. Many families are going on vacation next week.

2. I have offered to take care of their plants and pets.

3. I could be a part-time house-sitter.

 QUICK WRITE Write a paragraph about your favorite television show or movie. Include different verb tenses and tell which tense each verb is.

Grammar

RULE 6

Progressive Forms

- The present-progressive form tells about an action that is continuing now. Use *am*, *is*, or *are* followed by a present participle.

  Lila is reading a magazine.   *I am hoping to borrow it later.*

- The past-progressive form tells about an action that was continuing at an earlier time. Use the helping verb *was* or *were* and a present participle.

  Ms. Dawson's class was watching a classic film.

Practice: Write each sentence. Use the present-progressive or past-progressive form of the verb in parentheses. Choose the form that makes the most sense. Then circle the helping verbs.

1. Yesterday we _____ for school supplies. (shop)

2. Tom _____ for new folders and pens. (look)

3. My brothers _____ me find paper, crayons, and pencils. (help)

RULE 7

Perfect Tenses

- The present-perfect tense tells about an action that happened in the past. It also tells about an action that began in the past and is continuing in the present. Use the helping verb *have* or *has* followed by a past participle, which is usually the *-ed* form of a verb.

  I have finished my assignment.   *Jantelle has quizzed me.*

- The past-perfect tense tells about one past action that occurred before another past action. Use the helping verb *had* and a past participle.

  Before 1998, Jantelle had worked as a student teacher.

Practice: Write each sentence. Use the present-perfect or past-perfect tense of the verb in parentheses.

1. I've noticed that school spirit _____ in recent years. (increase)

2. Students _____ favorably to the teachers' support. (react)

3. The teacher _____ in this effort. (help)

RULE 8 — Linking Verbs

- Some verbs do not express action. These are called linking verbs.

   School is great.   *We are happy about the coming year.*

- A linking verb links the subject with a word in the predicate. This word can be a predicate noun, which renames or identifies the subject, or a predicate adjective, which describes the subject.

   My new teacher is Mrs. Dolce.   *Mrs. Dolce is patient.*

Common Linking Verbs				
am	was	being	feel	smell
is	were	been	appear	stay
are	be	seem	become	taste

Practice: Write the linking verb and the predicate noun or the predicate adjective in each sentence. Write *PN* for predicate noun and *PA* for predicate adjective.

1. That school is Afton Academy.

2. The students are very talented.

3. Their drama courses seem challenging.

RULE 9 — Irregular Verbs

- Irregular verbs do not add *-ed* to form the past tense and past participles. They are different from regular verbs.

   She sang.   *She has sung.*

Practice: Write each sentence. Use the correct verb in parentheses ( ) to complete each sentence.

1. The class (gone, went) to the beach.

2. They (saw, seen) some little fish in a tide pool.

3. Elvira (catched, caught) three fish for her aquarium.

 QUICK WRITE Make a chart that shows tenses of ten verbs. Write them in the present-progressive and past-progressive tenses.

Grammar

Personal Pronouns: Singular and Plural

- A **pronoun** is a word that takes the place of one or more nouns.

  The garden is beautiful.   *It is beautiful.*

- A **personal pronoun** can be singular or plural.

  Dave gave the seeds to Mom.   *He gave the seeds to Mom.*

  Dave and Lee gave the seeds to Dad. *They gave the seeds to Dad.*

Personal Pronouns

Singular	I	me	you	he, she, it	him, her, it
Plural	we	us	you	they	them

Practice: **Write each sentence. Replace the words in parentheses ( ) with a personal pronoun.**

1. (Jeff and I) planted peas, carrots, and onions in the garden.

2. (Susan and Mary) are in charge of watering the garden.

3. All of us are enjoying (this garden).

Pronouns and Referents

- A **referent**, or **antecedent**, of a **pronoun** is the word or group of words to which the pronoun refers.

  Blaise Pascal invented a calculator in 1642, and it was a great success.   *(pronoun = it, referent = calculator)*

Practice: **Write the pronoun in each sentence. Then write the referent, or the noun to which the pronoun refers.**

1. Pascal's father used a calculator to help him figure out tax payments.

2. Some people used pebbles to help them keep accurate records.

3. In the Middle Ages, merchants used tally sticks as they bought and sold goods.

RULE 3

Subject, Object, and Indefinite Pronouns

- A **subject pronoun** can take the place of a noun that is the subject of a sentence. *I, you, he, she, it, we,* and *they* are subject pronouns.

  Rex rides the bus.　　　*He rides the bus.*

- An **object pronoun** can be used as the object of an action verb or after words such as *to, for, with, in,* or *at.* The words *me, you, him, her, it, us,* and *them* are object pronouns.

  Rex talks to Bob.　　　*Rex talks to him.*

- An **indefinite pronoun**, such as *anyone, nobody,* or *both,* does not refer to a particular person, place, or thing.

Practice: Write each sentence. Underline each pronoun and say whether it is a subject, object, or indefinite pronoun.

1. Everyone is waiting for the bus.

2. Mom gives the fare to me.

3. When the bus arrives, we get on board.

RULE 4

Pronoun-Verb Agreement

- Sometimes a **pronoun** is used as the subject of a sentence. The verb must always agree with the subject pronoun.

  He watches basketball alone.　　*They watch basketball together.*

Practice: Write each sentence. Choose the verb in parentheses ( ) that agrees with the subject pronoun in the sentence.

1. We (are, is) in the school orchestra.

2. They (plays, play) the drums.

3. She (has, have) been playing the clarinet for about a year.

151

RULE 1

Adjectives

- An **adjective** describes, or modifies, a noun or pronoun. It may come before or after the word it describes. A single noun can be modified by more than one adjective.

  The roller coaster was huge.

  The huge, metal roller coaster was there.

- **Adjectives** describe, or modify, nouns or pronouns in three ways. They can explain *what kind*, *which one*, or *how many*.

  I enjoy the long rides.   *(What kind of rides?)*

  That ride is my favorite.   *(Which ride?)*

  I have ridden it seven times.   *(How many times?)*

- A **predicate adjective** follows a linking verb. It modifies the subject.

  That roller coaster is scary!

Practice: **Write the adjective or adjectives in each sentence.**

1. Airplanes are a wonderful form of transportation.
2. Many people fly on large jets.
3. These enormous jets can cross the ocean in a few hours.
4. Airplanes are quieter than they were many years ago.
5. They have comfortable seats and entertaining movies.

RULE 2

Articles: *a, an, the*

- **Articles** are special adjectives that you often use before nouns. The three articles are *a*, *an*, and *the*.

  The children asked for a piece of pie.

- Use *a* and *an* with singular nouns. Use *a* if the next word starts with a consonant sound. Use *an* if the next word starts with a vowel sound.

  She didn't want an apple. She said she wanted a sweet dessert.

- Use *the* to name a certain person, place, or thing.

  I'll have to check the pantry.

152

Practice: Write each sentence. Choose the correct article for each blank. Underline the adjectives.

1. I've been reading _____ book of classical mythology.

2. _____ stories take place in beautiful Greece.

3. Someday I'll take _____ trip to this fascinating place.

RULE 3

Demonstrative Adjectives

- **Demonstrative adjectives** point out particular persons or objects and tell *which one* or *which ones*. Demonstrative adjectives are *this*, *that*, *these*, and *those*.

- Use *this* and *that* with singular nouns. Use *this* to point out a person or object that is nearby. Use *that* to point out a person or object that is farther away.

  That Ferris wheel over there is the tallest in the country.

  This rocket ride over here shoots straight up in the air.

- Use *these* and *those* with plural nouns. Use *these* to point out people or objects that are nearby. Use *those* to point out people or objects that are farther away.

  These straps next to you hold you tight.

  Those two rides at the far end are also fantastic!

Practice: Write each sentence using the correct demonstrative adjective.

1. Elise, (this, these) pictures from your vacation are fantastic!

2. I love (that, those) one of the famous statue.

3. Where did you take (this, those) pictures to be developed?

 QUICK WRITE Write a journal entry describing a place you once visited. Use at least five adjectives. Underline each one.

Grammar

RULE 4

Comparative and Superlative Adjectives

- **Adjectives** can be used to compare two or more people, places, things, or ideas.

- A **comparative adjective** is made by adding *-er* to most one-syllable and some two-syllable adjectives.

  My sister is taller than my brother.

- A **superlative adjective** compares more than two things. You usually form the superlative by adding *-est*.

  My mother is the tallest person in our family.

Practice: Rewrite each sentence, changing the adjective or adjectives in parentheses ( ) to its comparative or superlative form.

1. I have three sisters, and the (little) one is five.

2. She is (friendly) in the morning than she is at night.

3. I know that I have the (cute) sisters in the world.

RULE 5

Comparing with *More* and *Most*

- To form **comparative** and **superlative adjectives** of most words with two or more syllables, use *more* and *most* instead of adding *-er* and *-est*.

  delicious   more delicious   most delicious

- Use *more* to form **comparative adjectives**. Use *most* to form **superlative adjectives**. Never use *more* and *most* before adjectives with *-er* and *-est* endings.

  Incorrect: *This book is more bigger than that one*

  Correct: *This book is bigger than that one.*

Practice: Write each sentence. Use the correct form of the adjective.

1. The (more, most) enormous animal at City Zoo is the gorilla.

2. Big Joe is also the (more, most) amusing animal at the zoo.

3. He makes (more, most) humorous faces than the chimps do.

Grammar

RULE 6

Comparing with *Good* and *Bad*

- The comparative and superlative forms of some adjectives are irregular. *Good* and *bad* are two irregular adjectives. The chart below shows how to use these words.

Adjective	Comparative	Superlative
good	better	best
bad	worse	worst

Practice: Write each sentence. Choose the correct form of *good* or *bad*.

1. Ray likes the ocean (best, better) than the lake.

2. He thinks the (best, better) part of the ocean is the waves.

3. He also believes the sand is a (best, good) place to play.

RULE 7

Combining Sentences: Adjectives

- Combine short, choppy sentences that tell about the same person, place, or thing. You can combine sentences by leaving out repeated words and adding an adjective to one of the sentences.

　　Choppy:　　*The elephant is large. The elephant is impressive.*

　　Combined:　*The elephant is large and impressive.*

Practice: Combine the two sentences into one sentence. Then underline the adjectives.

1. A Venus's-flytrap is a fascinating plant. A Venus's-flytrap is a unique plant.

2. This type of plant needs a dry place. This type of plant needs a sunny place.

3. This plant eats live bugs. This plant eats flying bugs.

 QUICK WRITE　Write a description of a person, place, or object that you think is fascinating. Use comparative and superlative adjectives.

Grammar

RULE 5

Possessive Pronouns

- **A possessive pronoun shows who or what owns something.**

  Blane's house is on the corner.   *His house is on the corner.*

- *My, your, his, her, its, our,* and *their* are possessive pronouns that come before nouns.

  Dad and I enjoyed your play.

- *Mine, yours, his, hers, its, ours,* and *theirs* are possessive pronouns that can stand alone.

  The camera on the stairs is mine.

Practice: Write each sentence. Replace the underlined word or words with the correct possessive pronoun.

1. The <u>children's</u> teacher is taking them on a field trip today.

2. <u>Terrence's</u> mom will go along as a chaperone.

3. <u>Ruthie's</u> dad is driving the bus to the museum.

RULE 1

Adverbs That Modify Verbs

- **An adverb can modify a verb.**

- **An adverb can supply three types of information about a verb:** *how, where,* or *when.*

  We arrived at the ocean today.
       (verb)   (when)

  Many fish swam nearby.   *Seagulls loudly squawked.*
       (verb)   (where)   (how)   (verb)

- **Many adverbs end in** *-ly.*

Practice: Write the adverb in each sentence. Write whether it tells *how, when,* or *where.*

1. We visited the ocean today.

2. Sharks swam briskly through the water.

3. One shark swam away.

RULE 2

Adverbs That Modify Adjectives and Adverbs

- **Adverbs** can modify adjectives.

    Nicole was very glad to see her cat.
    (adverb) (adjective)

- **Adverbs** can modify other adverbs.

    The cat leaped into the air quite rapidly.
    (adverb) (adverb)

Practice: Write the adverb and the adjective or adverb it modifies in each sentence.

1. Cats are seldom clumsy.

2. In fact, most cats are extremely agile.

3. A cat can leap surprisingly far.

RULE 3

Adverbs' Positions

- An **adverb** can come before or after the verb, adjective, or adverb it modifies or in another part of the sentence.

    The tourist behaved badly at the aquarium.
    (verb) (adverb)

    She was incredibly rude.
    (adverb) (adjective)

Practice: Write the verb, adjective, or adverb that the underlined adverb is modifying. Then write whether the underlined adverb comes before or after the word it is modifying.

1. Did you approach the shark's tank <u>carefully</u>?

2. Yes, we were <u>reasonably</u> cautious as we moved toward the tank.

3. The shark dipped <u>below</u>.

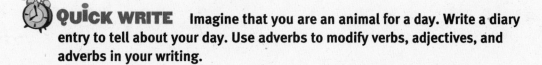 **QUICK WRITE**   Imagine that you are an animal for a day. Write a diary entry to tell about your day. Use adverbs to modify verbs, adjectives, and adverbs in your writing.

Grammar

 RULE 4

Negatives

- A **negative** is a word that means "no" or "not." Some examples of negatives are:

  no, not, never, barely, hardly, scarcely, don't, didn't, couldn't

- Do not use a **double negative** in one sentence. Correct a double negative by changing one negative into a positive word.

  Incorrect: *She didn't want no one to feel bad about the race.*

  Correct: *She didn't want anyone to feel bad about the race.*

Practice: Write each sentence correctly. Use only one negative in each sentence.

1. My brother didn't pick up no trash at the picnic.

2. He hasn't helped no one mow her yard.

3. He won't never earn a "Good Citizen" badge.

 RULE 5

Prepositions and Prepositional Phrases

- A **preposition** is a word that relates a noun or pronoun to another word in a sentence. Some common prepositions are:

  in, over, under, near, during, on, over, with, for, by, down

- A **prepositional phrase** begins with a preposition and ends with a noun or pronoun.

  A bat colony lives near the lake.

Practice: Write each sentence. Underline the prepositional phrases. Circle each preposition.

1. During the summer, Grandma and I bake every day.

2. Each afternoon we go to the store for supplies.

3. Our favorite little bakery is around the corner.

RULE 6

Prepositional Phrases: Adjectives and Adverbs

- Prepositional phrases act as adjectives when they modify or describe a noun or pronoun. These prepositional phrases are called adjective phrases. Adjective phrases answer the questions *What kind?* and *Which one?*

    The cow in the field is black.   (*Which cow is black?*)

- Prepositional phrases act as adverbs when they modify, or tell more about, verbs, adjectives, and adverbs. These prepositional phrases are called adverb phrases. Adverb phrases tell *where, how,* or *when.*

    The cow jumped over the fence.   (*Where did the cow jump?*)

Practice: Write each sentence. Underline the prepositional phrase. Write whether it is an adjective phrase or an adverb phrase.

1. The soccer match between the two championship teams will be exciting.

2. Everyone gets to the stadium early.

3. Dad and Marie have two good seats in left field.

4. Excitedly, they climb up the bleachers.

5. Tonight's game will begin at dark.

6. The Bears and the Redhawks are getting off the bus now.

7. The players near the clubhouse are starting to warm up.

8. That coach with the black T-shirt must be new.

9. The athletes and their trainers run onto the field.

10. The first kick rises into the air.

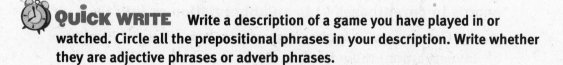

QUICK WRITE   Write a description of a game you have played in or watched. Circle all the prepositional phrases in your description. Write whether they are adjective phrases or adverb phrases.

Grammar

Titles and Names

- An *abbreviation* is a shortened form of a word. An *initial* is the first letter of a name. Titles and initials begin with a capital letter and end with a period.

Title	Abbreviation	Title	Abbreviation
Mister	Mr.	Senior	Sr.
Doctor	Dr.	Governor	Gov.

Name	Initials
John Robert Hayes	J. R. Hayes

Organizations

- In both formal and informal writing, use abbreviations for certain organizations and government agencies. These abbreviations usually have all capital letters and no periods.

  United Nations   UN   *Central Intelligence Agency*   CIA

Internet Addresses

- Use abbreviations at the end of Internet addresses.

commercial	.com	educational	.edu
organization	.org	network	.net

Practice Rewrite each sentence. Change each word or group of words in parentheses ( ) to an abbreviation or initials.

1. On Career Day, a spokesperson from the (Federal Bureau of Investigation) talked to our class.

2. (Doctor) (Andrew Joseph) Higgins also spoke.

3. (Woman) Margaret Lee told us about computer programming.

4. She invited us to e-mail her at www.data.(commercial).

5. Our last visitor was James Allen (Senior), a member of the (National Football League).

Units of Measure

- Abbreviate units of measure.

  in.—inch(es)   *ft.—foot (feet)*   *g—gram(s)*   *L—liter(s)*

Time

- Abbreviations to indicate time before noon (A.M., for *ante meridiem*) and after noon (P.M., for *post meridiem*) are capitalized with periods after each letter.

- Abbreviations for years are capitalized with periods: B.C. for *before Christ* and A.D. for *Anno Domini*, "in the year of the Lord."

Days and Months

- In informal writing, use abbreviations of the days of the week and the months of the year. These abbreviations begin with a capital letter and end with a period. May, June, and July are never abbreviated.

Day	Abbreviation	Month	Abbreviation
Monday	Mon.	January	Jan.
Tuesday	Tues.	February	Feb.
Wednesday	Wed.	March	Mar.
Thursday	Thurs.	April	Apr.
Friday	Fri.	August	Aug.
Saturday	Sat.	September	Sept.
Sunday	Sun.	October	Oct.
		November	Nov.
		December	Dec.

Practice Write each sentence using abbreviations.

1. Meet me on Thursday, September 15, at three in the afternoon.

2. Shannon measures five feet and ten inches tall.

3. Roman Emperor Tiberius lived from 42 before Christ to 37 Anno Domini.

Grammar

Addresses

- Address abbreviations are capitalized and followed by a period.

Avenue	Ave.	Drive	Dr.
Street	St.	Road	Rd.
Boulevard	Blvd.	Post Office	P. O.

States

- **United States Postal Service** abbreviations for the names of states consist of two capital letters. No period follows these abbreviations.

State	Abbreviation	State	Abbreviation
Alabama	AL	Montana	MT
Alaska	AK	Nebraska	NE
Arizona	AZ	Nevada	NV
Arkansas	AR	New Hampshire	NH
California	CA	New Jersey	NJ
Colorado	CO	New Mexico	NM
Connecticut	CT	New York	NY
Delaware	DE	North Carolina	NC
Florida	FL	North Dakota	ND
Georgia	GA	Ohio	OH
Hawaii	HI	Oklahoma	OK
Idaho	ID	Oregon	OR
Illinois	IL	Pennsylvania	PA
Indiana	IN	Rhode Island	RI
Iowa	IA	South Carolina	SC
Kansas	KS	South Dakota	SD
Kentucky	KY	Tennessee	TN
Louisiana	LA	Texas	TX
Maine	ME	Utah	UT
Maryland	MD	Vermont	VT
Massachusetts	MA	Virginia	VA
Michigan	MI	Washington	WA
Minnesota	MN	West Virginia	WV
Mississippi	MS	Wisconsin	WI
Missouri	MO	Wyoming	WY

First Words in Sentences

- Capitalize the first word of a sentence.

  Soil provides nutrients for plants.

- Capitalize the first word of a direct quotation. Do not capitalize the second part of an interrupted quotation.

  "I am leaving," Jan declared, "as soon as I can."

- When the second part of a quotation is a new sentence, put a period after the interrupting expression and capitalize the first word of the new sentence.

  "I know that song," said Lisa. "We learned it last week."

Salutations and Closings

- Capitalize all words in a letter's greeting, including the title and name of the person addressed.

  Dear Sirs: *Dear Friend,*   *Dear Uncle Jim,*

- Capitalize the first word in the closing of a letter.

  Sincerely,   *Yours truly,*   *Fondly,*

Practice Rewrite this friendly letter correctly. Use capital letters where needed, and abbreviate when possible.

(1)   49 Wilshire Boulevard

(2)   Dedham, Massachusetts 02062

(3)   January 30, 2010

(4) dear grandma joyce,

(5) here is a poem for you. **(6)** It's my way of saying, "happy birthday!"

Another year older

Isn't so bad.

(7) you look terrific,

Even better than Dad!

(8) your grandson,

Gregory

163

Grammar

Proper Nouns: Names and Titles of People

- Capitalize the names of people and the initials that stand for their names.

    Alice Suzanne Martin   *A. S. Martin*

- Capitalize titles or abbreviations of titles when they come before or after the names of people.

    Mrs. Kate Jones   *General K. T. Jones*   *Dr. Albert Garcia*

- Capitalize an official title when it appears before a person's name or when it is used in a direct address.

    When we had a hurricane, we contacted Governor Winslow.

    Governor Winslow, you have a call on line 7.

- Do not capitalize the title that falls after or is a substitute for a person's name.

    Frances Smith, the mayor of our city, called for help.

- Capitalize words that show family relationships when used as titles or as substitutes for a person's name.

    Then Dad and Grandma Ellen cooked dinner.

- Do not capitalize words that show family relationships when they are preceded by a possessive noun or pronoun.

    Diane's grandmother is a good cook. Her dad is a good cook, too.

- Capitalize the abbreviations Jr. and Sr.

    Robert James, Jr.   *Marvin Robbins, Sr.*

- Capitalize the pronoun *I*.

    Can I help cook dinner?

Practice Rewrite each sentence correctly. Capitalize the names and titles of people where needed.

1. The Arbor Day committee is led by p. j. winslow.

2. We contacted mayor henry erickson about planting trees.

3. He asked us to call dr. mario ortiz, the city's landscaper.

4. Dr. Ortiz referred us to deputy mayor nina grayson.

5. The deputy mayor sent mr. price to help us organize our project.

6. P. J. and i bought a tree with the Arbor Day committee funds.

7. P. J. Martin, sr. delivered the tree to the park.

8. I helped uncle joe dig the hole.

9. My uncle and i worked hard.

10. I watched as P. J. Martin, jr. planted the tree and watered it.

Proper Nouns: Names of Places

- Capitalize the names of cities, states, countries, and continents. Do not capitalize articles or prepositions that are part of the name.

City	*New York City*
State	*Florida*
Country	*United States of America*
Continent	*North America*

- Capitalize the names of bodies of water and geographical features.

  Atlantic Ocean   *Niagara Falls*   *Grand Canyon*

- Capitalize the names of sections of the country.

  the South   *the Pacific Northwest*

- Do not capitalize compass points when they just show direction.

  New York is east of Cleveland.

- Capitalize the names of streets and highways.

  Dover Street   *Santa Ana Freeway*

- Capitalize the names of buildings, bridges, and monuments.

  Sears Tower   *Brooklyn Bridge*   *Jefferson Memorial*

- Capitalize the names of stars and planets.

  The closest star to our planet is Proxima Centauri.

  The planet closest to the sun is Mercury.

- Capitalize *Earth* when it refers to the planet. Do not capitalize *earth* when preceded by *the*. Do not capitalize sun or moon.

  One moon revolves around Earth.

  The earth revolves around the sun.

Practice **Rewrite each sentence correctly. Use capital letters where needed.**

1. Our class visited arnold arboretum, which is south of boston, massachusetts.

2. The bus passed boston harbor, and we saw the atlantic ocean.

3. We drove along washington street and arborway until we arrived.

4. On the tour, we learned about trees in north america.

5. The tour guide said that earth is the only planet in our solar system with plant life.

Grammar

Other Proper Nouns and Adjectives

- Capitalize the names of schools, clubs, organizations, institutions, political parties, and businesses.

  Jefferson Middle School   *Girl Scouts of America*

  Hopewell Chamber of Commerce   *Smithsonian Institution*

- Capitalize the names of historic events, periods of time, and documents.

  Battle of Bunker Hill   *Colonial Period*

  Declaration of Independence

- Capitalize the days of the week, months of the year, and holidays. Do not capitalize the names of the seasons.

  We started school on Tuesday, September 1.

  Our first holiday is on Labor Day.

  My favorite season is autumn.

- Capitalize abbreviations that are parts of a proper noun.

  Dr.   *Ave.*   *Oct.*   *Ln.*

- Capitalize the names of ethnic groups, nationalities, and languages.

  Many people in our town are Norwegian.

  I speak Japanese.

- Capitalize proper adjectives that are formed from the names of ethnic groups and nationalities.

  Italian bread   *Egyptian cotton*

- Capitalize the first word of each main topic and subtopic in an outline.

  I. Products and exports

  A. Natural resources

  B. Manufactured goods

Practice Rewrite each sentence correctly. Use capital letters where needed.

1. The sixth graders at park middle school studied ancient Greece.

2. The parkville history club and its president, mr. Gary Post, talked to the class.

3. The students learned about the trojan war.

4. The students learned that some anthropologists have been studying what Greece was like during the bronze age.

5. The greek empire once stretched all the way to India.

Titles of Works

- Capitalize the first, last, and all important words in the title of a book, play, short story, poem, film, article, newspaper, magazine, TV series, chapter of a book, or song.

> I can't wait to read *Roll of Thunder, Hear My Cry*.
>
> Did you see *Peter Pan* at the community theater?
>
> A clever short story is "Rip van Winkle."
>
> My favorite poem when I was young was "Old King Cole."
>
> You should read "Cars of the Future" in this month's *Vehicles Monthly*.
>
> My dad reads *The Los Angeles Times*.
>
> Did you watch *Newsbreaker* last night?
>
> Chapter one of that book is titled "The Long Night."
>
> I sang the "Star-Spangled Banner" before the big game.

Practice Rewrite each sentence correctly. Capitalize all titles of works.

1. Did you read *white fang* by Jack London?
2. Yes, my favorite chapter was "the gray cub."
3. Scott reminds me of the main character in the film *old yeller*.
4. If the story were true, we would surely have read about it in *dog lovers monthly*.
5. They would probably title the article "man: dog's worst friend."
6. If I were going to write a play based on the book, I would call it *wolf dog*.
7. However, if I were to write a poem about the story, I would title it "gentle inside."
8. Let's write a humorous short story about a sled dog and call it "rush and mush."
9. We could write a funny song about a sled dog and call it "bobsled blues."
10. Maybe we could perform the song on that television show called *singing for dollars*.

Grammar

End Punctuation

- Use end punctuation at the end of a sentence.
- A period ends a declarative sentence. A declarative sentence makes a statement.

  I have a cold.

- A period or an exclamation mark ends an imperative sentence. An imperative sentence makes a command or a request.

  Don't do that! Keep yourself warm.

- A question mark ends an interrogative sentence. An interrogative sentence asks a question.

  Will I get well?

- An exclamation mark ends an exclamatory sentence. An exclamatory sentence expresses strong emotion.

  I finally feel better!

Periods

- Use a period at the end of an abbreviation.

  Dr.   St.   Tues.   Jan.

- Use a period in abbreviations for time (in both formal and informal writing).

  12:00 A.M.   12:00 P.M.

- Use a period after initials.

  P. J. Reynolds

- Use a period after numbers and letters in an outline.

  I. Margaret Mead
  *   A. Famous anthropologist*
  *   B. Summary of her work*

Hyphens

- Use a hyphen or hyphens in certain compound words.

  drive-in   merry-go-round

- Use a hyphen to show the division of a word at the end of a line. Always divide the word between syllables.

  Jennifer wants to go camping and canoe-
  ing this weekend.

- Use a hyphen in compound numbers.

  twenty-two students   forty-nine stairs

Grammar

Colons and Semicolons

- Use a **colon** to separate the hour and the minute when you write the time of day.

  12:45   *1:15*   *6:30*

- Use a colon after the greeting of a business letter.

  Dear Sirs: *Dear Mr. Franklin:*

- Use a colon to introduce a list of items that ends a sentence. Do not use a colon if the list immediately follows a verb or a preposition. Leave out the colon or reword the sentence.

  You will need these items: swimsuit, towel, and sandals.

  The items you will need are a swimsuit, a towel, and sandals.

- Use a **semicolon** to join parts of a compound sentence when a conjunction is not used.

  I do the homework; Rick has the fun.

Apostrophes

- Use an **apostrophe** and an *s* (*'s*) to form the possessive of a singular noun and to form the possessive of a plural noun that does not end in *s*.

  Jason's book   *my mom's bike*   *the car's horn*

- Use an apostrophe alone to form the possessive of a plural noun that ends in *s*.

  ladies' purses   *donkeys' brays*   *lilies' scent*

- Use an apostrophe in a contraction to show where a letter or letters are missing.

  we + are = we're   *he + is = he's*   *would + not = wouldn't*

- Do not use an apostrophe in a possessive pronoun.

  its good points   *their friends*   *your idea*

Practice Rewrite each sentence correctly. Add punctuation where needed.

1. He found these childrens toys near the merry go round one bat two balls one mitt

2. Our group will meet at 830 AM your group wont meet until 230 PM

3. Why did Dr Riviera move my sisters appointment ahead twenty eight days

Grammar

Commas

- Use a comma between the name of the city and state in an address.

  Lafayette, Indiana

- Use a comma after the name of a state or a country when it is used with the name of a city in a sentence.

  We visited San Francisco, California, on our vacation.

- Use a comma between the day and year in a date.

  April 20, 2002   July 4, 1776

- Use a comma before and after the year when it is used with both the month and the day in a sentence. Do not use a comma if only the month and the year are given.

  June 4, 2000, is our last day of school.

  The school was built in September 2001.

- Use a comma after the greeting in a friendly letter and after the closing in all letters.

  Dear Tyler,   Sincerely,

- Use commas to separate three or more items in a series.

  Our flag is red, white, and blue.

  You are kind, patient, and helpful.

- Use a comma before *and, but,* or *or* when it joins simple sentences to form a compound sentence.

  We like to play softball, but the field is often used.

  My mother can drive us, or we can take the bus.

  My brownies are tasty, and everyone enjoys them.

Practice Rewrite the following friendly letter. Place commas where needed.

365 Harding Drive

1. La Grange Illinois

2. December 4 2001

3. Dear Tomiko

4. On December 16 2001 I will start winter break.

5. Yours truly

Jennifer

Grammar

Commas

- Use two **commas** to set off an **appositive**, a group of words that tells more about the subject.

  Joe, a good student, enjoys science class.

- Use a comma after introductory words or phrases in a sentence.

  Yes, I enjoy science class.

- Use a comma to set off a noun of direct address.

  Greta, please pass the mustard.

- Use a comma to set off a direct quotation.

  "I'll be right there," I said.

  "Will you please," I added, "pass the salt?"

- Use two commas to set off words that interrupt the flow of thought in a sentence.

  There is, no doubt, room for another bike in the garage.

- Use commas after a long prepositional phrase or series of phrases at the beginning of a sentence.

  At the end of the meeting, we took a vote.

- Use a comma before the word *too* when it means "also."

  I want to go to the park, too.

Practice Rewrite each sentence. Add commas where needed.

1. Patty what is your favorite subject?

2. Oh I like math the best.

3. Mathematics the study of numbers is very interesting to me.

4. Well I'm fond of a different subject.

5. "Physical science the study of matter is my favorite subject" said Nancy.

6. If possible can you please tell us where the hayride will be?

7. To the south of town, over the bridge is the stable called Shady Acres.

8. As you know nothing will stop us from going.

9. Craig wants to join us too.

10. He will of course be invited.

Grammar

Quotation Marks

- Use quotation marks before and after a direct quotation, the exact words that a speaker says.

  "Someday I'm going to learn to roller blade," said Paul.

  "Someday," said Paul, "I'm going to learn to roller blade."

- Use a comma or commas to separate a phrase, such as *he said*, from the quotation itself. Place the comma outside the opening quotation marks but inside the closing quotation marks.

  Veronica asked, "What would you like to learn to do?"

  "This summer," replied Adam, "I'd like to learn to roller blade."

- Place a period inside closing quotation marks.

  Pam added, "I want to learn to snorkel."

- Place a question mark or an exclamation mark inside the quotation marks when it is part of the quotation.

  "What do you want to learn to do?" asked Maria.

  "I want to figure out how to get straight A's, of course!" shouted Lily.

Practice Rewrite each sentence correctly. Add punctuation where needed.

1. Are you ready for Adventure Camp asked Mr. Lee.

2. I'm ready for sailing said Courtney.

3. Will we asked Keiko get to ride horses?

4. Yes replied Mr. Lee we will.

5. Lionel said How great this camp is!

Quotation Marks

- Use quotation marks around the title of a short story, essay, song, short poem, magazine or newspaper article, and a chapter of a book.

  "Jack and the Beanstalk"   "Yankee Doodle Dandy"

  "How Valentine's Day Came to Be"   "Little Miss Muffet"

  "Hurricane Floyd Rocks the Southeast"   "A Mysterious Visitor"

Practice Rewrite each sentence correctly. Add quotation marks where needed.

1. Should we sing Let Me Call You Sweetheart at the Valentine's Day assembly?

2. Perhaps we should read a funny poem, such as Georgie Porgie.

3. Or, we could read and act out a magazine article, such as this one titled Ten Ways to Be Sweet.

4. It might be fun to act out the chapter of the book called True Friends.

5. I think the best idea is to write and read aloud an essay titled What Valentine's Day Means to Us.

Italics (Underlining)

- Use italics or underlining to enclose the title of a book, film, play, television series, magazine, or newspaper.

The Secret Garden	The Secret Garden
Air Bud	Air Bud
The Price Is Right	The Price Is Right
Fiddler on the Roof	Fiddler on the Roof
Family Circle	Family Circle
The Chicago Tribune	The Chicago Tribune

Practice Rewrite each sentence correctly. Underline titles where needed.

1. Are you going to see SpaceForce at Movieland this weekend?

2. No, I'm staying home to watch Lion's Den on television.

3. Are you still reading The Lion, the Witch, and the Wardrobe?

4. Yes, and I like reading the sports section of The Los Angeles Times, too.

5. Did you want to borrow my copy of Sports Illustrated for Kids?

Grammar

Sentence Structure: Diagramming

A **sentence diagram** is a visual method of showing how the words, phrases, and clauses in a sentence go together. A diagram always begins with the most important parts of the sentence.

Simple Subjects and Simple Predicates

- Begin a sentence diagram by drawing a horizontal line. This is called the base line. Draw a vertical line separating the base line in two.
- Write the simple subject of the sentence on the left and the simple predicate on the right. Include helping verbs with the main verb.

Starfish live in shallow water.   *They are found in all the oceans.*

| Starfish | live | | They | are found |

- A sentence may have a compound subject, a compound predicate, or both. Each simple subject or predicate is placed on a separate horizontal line in the diagram. The word *and*, *or*, or *but* is placed on a dotted vertical line that connects the compound elements.

Snails, oysters, and clams are mollusks.   *Lobsters catch food and fight enemies with their claws.*

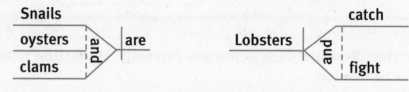

Practice Make a sentence diagram of the simple or compound subject and predicate in each sentence.

1. Stiff spines cover the body of a starfish.

2. Suction cups are attached to the feet of a starfish.

3. Walruses and otters are water mammals.

4. Mammals have backbones and breathe air.

5. Dolphins and porpoises have streamlined bodies and move gracefully in the water.

RULE 2

Direct Objects

- A **direct object** answers the question *whom* or *what* after the verb.
- In a sentence diagram, place the direct object on the base line, to the right of the simple predicate, or verb.
- Draw a vertical line separating the verb from the direct object. This line does *not* cross the base line.

Earth's gravity pulls all matter toward the ground.

Gravity | pulls | matter

Practice Make a sentence diagram of the simple subject, the simple predicate, and the direct object in each sentence.

1. Metals conduct electricity.
2. Liquids take the form of their containers.
3. Plants make their own food.
4. The heat of the sun warms Earth.
5. You hear many different sounds each day.

RULE 3

Indirect Objects

- An **indirect object** answers the question *to whom? for whom?* or *for what?* after an action verb.
- Place the indirect object on a horizontal line below and to the right of the verb. Use a slanted line to connect it to the verb.

Janet gave Robert some ideas for a science project.

Janet | gave | ideas
Robert

Practice Make a sentence diagram of the simple subject, simple predicate, indirect object, and direct object.

1. Caroline showed Darla a diagram of an eye.
2. Darla handed the teacher her homework.
3. The teacher gave the class a new assignment.
4. The optic nerve sends the brain a message.
5. Our eyes give us much information about the world.

Grammar

Grammar

RULE 4

Adjectives and Adverbs

- **Adjectives** modify or describe nouns and pronouns. Adjectives tell *what kind, which one(s)*, and *how many*. In a sentence diagram, place an adjective on a slanted line below the noun or pronoun it modifies.
- Diagram possessive nouns and pronouns and the articles *a, an,* and *the* in the same way you diagram other kinds of adjectives.

That girl's collection includes two yellow frogs.

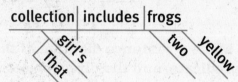

- **Adverbs** describe verbs, adjectives, or other adverbs. Adverbs tell *how, when, where,* or *to what extent.*
- In a sentence diagram, place an adverb on a slanted line below the word it modifies.

Beetles can live almost anywhere.

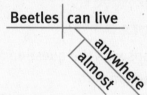

Practice **Diagram each sentence.**

1. Most frogs have thin, moist skin.

2. Male frogs make loud, croaking sounds.

3. A frog has a long, sticky tongue.

4. A frog has very strong back legs.

5. Frogs can swim very well.

6. This beetle has brightly colored wings.

7. Wild chimpanzees sometimes use tools.

8. The huge gorilla ate a ripe, yellow banana.

9. Jackrabbits can run very fast.

10. Wild mice hardly ever enter houses.

Grammar

 RULE 5

Predicate Nouns and Predicate Adjectives

- In a sentence diagram, place the predicate noun or predicate adjective on the base line, to the right of the simple predicate, or verb.
- Draw a slanted line separating the verb from the predicate noun or predicate adjective. This line does not cross the base line.
- The slanted line indicates that the word refers back to the subject, either renaming it or describing it.

Sandra is a good student.

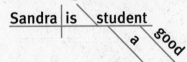

Practice **Diagram each sentence.**

1. Sandra's favorite book is *Oliver Twist*.
2. Oliver was a poor orphan boy.
3. The poor child was often hungry.
4. Oliver's life was very difficult.
5. Oliver's new friends were not quite respectable.
6. Fagin was a sly old thief.
7. Oliver was actually a rich man's son.
8. Oliver's mother was Agnes Fleming.
9. The author is Charles Dickens.
10. Sandra's copy is a library book.

Grammar

Prepositional Phrases

- A **prepositional phrase** is a group of words that modifies other words in a sentence. In a sentence diagram, write the preposition on a slanted line below the word it modifies. Place the object of the preposition on a horizontal line. In the following sentence, *on the windowsill* is the prepositional phrase that acts as an adjective modifying the noun *cat*.

The cat on the windowsill purred contentedly.

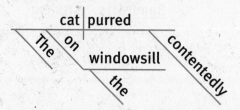

- A prepositional phrase can also be used as an adverb. In the following sentence, *on the windowsill* modifies the verb *napped*.

The cat napped on the windowsill.

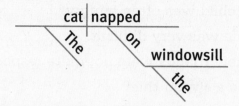

Practice **Diagram every word in these sentences.**

1. Most plants reproduce from seeds.
2. The smell of the flowers attracts bees.
3. The shape of a tropical orchid attracts wasps.
4. Pollen gets on the insects' bodies.
5. The insects fly to the next flower.

Compound Sentences

- A compound sentence has two or more independent clauses joined by a coordinating conjunction, such as *and, but,* or *or.*

- When you diagram a compound sentence, join the independent clauses in the following way:

    The bulbs are planted in the fall, and the flowers appear in the early spring.

    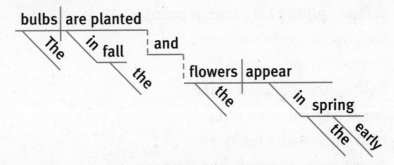

- In a sentence diagram, the second part of the compound sentence is always placed below the first part.

Practice Diagram every word in these compound sentences.

1. Tulips look like bells, and they come in different colors.

2. Some tulips are solid colors, and others have streaks of different colors.

3. Most tulips have six petals, but some can have double rows of petals.

4. You may see flowers along a quiet path, or you may find them in an empty lot.

5. Some flowers are planted by people, but wildflowers grow on their own.

6. Many wildflowers are annuals, and they live for one year.

7. Some people pick wildflowers, and many kinds have become rare.

8. Some orchids grow in hot, damp climates, but other types grow in cool woods.

9. Most orchids are grown for their beautiful flowers, but one kind of orchid is used for food.

10. Vanilla comes from a vanilla orchid, and this flavoring is used in many foods.

Extra Practice

Sentences and Sentence Fragments

A. Write whether each sentence is a complete sentence or a sentence fragment.

1. Fun things to do during the summer.

2. We went swimming at the pool today.

3. Jumped off the high diving board.

4. Kelly wore a new swimsuit.

5. Floated on my back.

6. Next to the lifeguard stand.

7. Jacob learned to do a flip.

8. Hold my breath underwater.

9. Towel, snorkel, mask, and flippers.

10. You should always wear sunscreen.

B. Rewrite each pair of fragments as a complete sentence.

11. Yesterday we. Went to the park to play baseball.

12. Lydia. Hit the first home run of the game.

13. The players. Were very hot and thirsty.

14. Just then, an ice cream truck. Drove by the ballpark.

15. Joey's dog, Peanut. Likes to catch the fly balls.

16. Rebecca, the girl with red hair. Pitched the first three innings.

17. After the sixth inning, the score. Was tied at 3 to 3.

18. My friend, Sam. Borrowed my glove.

19. Before long, the sun. Began to set.

20. Baseball. Is a great summer activity.

C. Complete each sentence fragment.

21. Playing baseball.

22. Hot in the sun.

23. Drank lemonade.

24. A dip in the pool.

25. Summer.

Kinds of Sentences

A. **Write whether each sentence is declarative, interrogative, imperative, or exclamatory.**

1. I went on vacation with my family.

2. Where did you go?

3. Please tell me about your trip.

4. How much fun we had!

5. First, we went to a space museum.

6. What an amazing trip that was!

7. Did you meet any astronauts?

8. Look at this picture of the astronauts.

9. Next, we looked at all the stars in the planetarium.

10. How bright the stars are!

B. **Write each sentence with the correct end punctuation.**

11. Did you see any constellations

12. I saw the Big Dipper and Orion

13. What a great vacation we had

14. Tell me what else you saw

15. After the museum, we went to the zoo

16. Did you see the elephants

17. We saw the tigers, too

18. Oh, I love the tigers

19. Come with us next time

20. Tell me when you plan to go again

C. **Write the sentences. Add the correct punctuation at the end of each sentence. Then write what type of sentence it is.**

21. I learned a lot of new things on my vacation

22. What an exciting trip it was

23. Where are you going next time

24. Give me a clue

25. We are going hiking and camping

Extra Practice

Combining Sentences: Compound Sentences

A. Write which sentences are simple sentences and which are compound sentences.

1. I will visit camp in Colorado in June.

2. I didn't want to go at first, but then I read the camp brochure.

3. My group will sleep in a big log cabin near the lake.

4. The counselors build a big fire, and the campers cook fish.

5. There are many fascinating activities at camp.

6. I will learn to paddle a canoe this year.

7. I like photography, and many plants are around the camp.

8. My friends will take pictures, and we can make a scrapbook.

9. Oh, how exciting it is to hike in the mountains!

10. Jake was going to camp, but he decided to work for his dad.

B. Write each sentence. Write *S* for simple sentences and *C* for compound sentences. Underline the conjunctions.

11. I started a dog-walking business, and I had a lot of fun.

12. I helped many people, and I made some money, too.

13. I sent out advertisements about my services.

14. I did not get many phone calls at first, but I did not give up.

15. I walked around, and I noticed the neighbors with dogs.

16. I knocked on the door at every house.

17. I introduced myself, or I left a business card.

18. I got a lot of responses, and I was happy.

19. I asked my neighbor Sara to work with me, and she said yes.

20. We fed the dogs twice a day.

C. Rewrite each pair of simple sentences as a compound sentence. Add the conjunction that shows the correct meaning.

21. We walked ten dogs at once. Things did not always go smoothly.

22. One day, Sara tripped over a rock. All the dogs ran away.

23. Some dogs came right away. Others were hard to catch.

24. Sara may walk dogs again this summer. She may not.

25. Having a business can be fun. It can also be a lot of responsibility.

Combining Sentences: Complex Sentences

A. Write the dependent clause in each sentence.

1. Before class began, Jason told me about his new computer.

2. He can play games on it although he uses it mostly for research.

3. Jason would play all day if his parents would let him.

4. After we talked, I decided to learn about computers.

5. Since I was at school, I borrowed a book from the library.

6. While I read, I learned about the invention of the first computer.

7. This computer was fairly fast although it was invented in 1888.

8. When a census was done, the computer was a great asset.

9. Because the computer was so successful, the inventor sold it.

10. After the computer was invented, the world changed.

B. Write the sentences. Draw one line under the dependent clause in each sentence. Draw two lines under the conjunction.

11. Though I read the book slowly, some parts were confusing.

12. After I used the mouse for a while, I really started to like it.

13. The first electronic computer was as big as a house, while today's computers can be smaller than your hand.

14. Until I read the book, I didn't know about the first computers.

15. The first successful one ran in 1946, before my dad was born.

16. Because it was so large, it weighed more than 30 tons.

17. Newer computers were faster, although they were still large.

18. Since businesses had to store data, they began to use computers.

19. When computer prices dropped, people bought them for home use.

20. After some time had passed, computers became even easier to use.

C. Form complex sentences by combining clauses.

21. As computers became easier to use. They became more popular.

22. As soon as personal computers were invented. Many people bought one.

23. Read a book about computers. If you want to know more.

24. If I can. I will find out more about the computer industry.

25. After school ends. I'm going to the computer store.

Extra Practice

Mechanics and Usage: Punctuating Sentences

A. Write the missing punctuation in each sentence.

1. Figure skating is my favorite sport at the winter Olympics

2. Did you see the winner in the solo competition

3. I watched the games last year but I missed them this year.

4. During the summer Olympics my favorite competition is soccer.

5. Come watch the game with me this year

6. Although it looks hard pole vaulting is interesting to watch.

7. Would you like to participate in the Olympics

8. Wow, that would be exciting

9. I would love to try figure skating but it looks difficult.

10. I may try figure skating anyway I think it would be a lot of fun.

B. Write each pair of clauses as one sentence.

11. After I eat dinner. I want to watch the winter Olympics.

12. Shawn's favorite Olympic sport is bobsledding. But he gets nervous watching it.

13. I could watch bobsledding. Or I could watch skiing.

14. While it is not usually my favorite. I enjoy watching skiing.

15. Roxanne's favorite is ice dancing. Because it is exciting.

16. There are a lot of twirls. And the skaters are energetic.

17. If it is possible. I would like to travel to the next winter Olympics.

18. Wherever the winter Olympics are held. It should be snowy.

19. The American team looks tired. As if everyone practiced too hard.

20. I want to watch the games again. Because they were so inspiring.

C. Write each pair of clauses as one sentence. Use conjunctions and commas where needed.

21. The American ice hockey team lost. It played a good game.

22. The Canadian players could win. The Swedish team beats them.

23. Whenever one team scored. The crowd went wild.

24. My sister wants to see the skating competition. I prefer the skiing.

25. I am looking forward to the downhill skiing. It is fun to watch.

Combining Sentences: Compound Subjects

A. **Write the compound subject in each sentence.**

1. Joe and Ana entered the race.

2. Jeremy and Tamara will cheer them on.

3. Marie or Keith will buy lemonade for everyone.

4. Renée and Dru made the sandwiches.

5. Tony or Shannon can make banners.

6. Donna and Carl heard thunder.

7. Lane and Corrine looked up at the rain.

8. The sandwiches and chips got wet.

9. Renée and Dru began packing up the food.

10. Tony and Shannon were disappointed.

B. **Write the simple subjects that can be joined to create a compound subject.**

11. Mark went to the race. Leslie went to the race.

12. The students cheered. The teachers cheered.

13. The runners were soaked. The coaches were soaked.

14. Lane thought the rain was funny. I thought the rain was funny.

15. Corrine took down the banners. Shannon took down the banners.

16. The banners were ruined. The signs were ruined.

17. The crowd escaped the rain. The runners escaped the rain.

18. Donna walked home. Carl walked home.

19. Jeremy ran all the way. I ran all the way.

20. Lee didn't see the race. Carolyn didn't see the race.

C. **Write each pair of sentences as one sentence with a compound subject.**

21. Joe sang in the rain. Ana sang in the rain.

22. Shannon can get a dry towel. Dru can get a dry towel.

23. Joe could have won the race. Ana could have won the race.

24. Sara played in the puddles. Sam played in the puddles.

25. Leslie went home after the race. I went home after the race.

Grammar

Combining Sentences: Compound Predicates

A. **Write the compound predicate in each sentence.**

1. Elaine petted and stroked Jared's dog.

2. The dog panted and licked Elaine's hand.

3. Jared's dog chased and caught the ball.

4. Jared will enter and show his dog in a dog competition.

5. The dog barked and whined before the show.

6. Jared brushed and groomed his dog.

7. Elaine watches and enjoys the dog show.

8. The dog escapes and runs from Jared.

9. Jared panics and runs after his dog.

10. Elaine looks and laughs at the loose dog.

B. **Write the simple predicates that can be joined to create a compound predicate.**

11. The big dog runs. The big dog chases the spectators.

12. The spectators watch the dog. The spectators follow the dog.

13. Jared yells at his dog. Jared whistles at his dog.

14. Elaine corners the excited dog. Elaine catches the excited dog.

15. The officials halt the show. The officials postpone the show.

16. The dog whines when caught. The dog growls when caught.

17. The scared spectators look. The scared spectators flee.

18. The dog's leash stretches. The dog's leash breaks.

19. Jared scolds his dog. Jared lectures his dog.

20. The tired dog sits on the grass. The tired dog plays on the grass.

C. **Write each pair of sentences as one with a compound predicate.**

21. The officials sigh with relief. The officials smile with relief.

22. Jared's dog sits up. Jared's dog begs.

23. Freddy laughs at the dog. Freddy points at the dog.

24. The spectators cheer for the dog. The spectators clap for the dog.

25. Jared wipes his forehead. Jared takes a bow.

Mechanics and Usage: Correcting Run-on Sentences

A. **Write the sentences. Draw a line between the two sentences that should be separated in each run-on sentence.**

1. Sandra went for a walk she wanted to see the city.

2. She saw people strolling they were smiling and talking.

3. Twins were walking their dog the dog was chasing squirrels.

4. Sandra saw some friends in the park they were playing a game.

5. She decided to join her friends they were happy to see her.

6. Sandra and her friends played Frisbee they formed two teams.

7. Sandra saw several people fly kites the kites were colorful.

8. Sandra was getting hungry she stopped for lunch.

9. The vendors smiled their food smelled good.

10. Sandra decided to buy a hot dog it was wrapped in foil.

B. **Write each run-on sentence as two simple sentences.**

11. Sandra met a girl at the park the girl was collecting pine cones.

12. The girl's name was Maria Sandra helped her find pine cones.

13. The pine cones were easy to find the girls put them in a bag.

14. Maria wanted to make a wreath she needed twenty pine cones.

15. Sandra found twelve pine cones Maria found eight.

16. Sandra and Maria said good-bye they planned to meet again.

17. Sandra fed the ducks some corn they were hungry.

18. The ducks quacked at Sandra the ducks wanted more food.

19. Jamie rode by on his skateboard he waved at Sandra.

20. Sandra smiled and waved she was glad to see Jamie.

C. **Correct each run-on sentence by making it a compound or complex sentence. Write the new sentence.**

21. Sandra started to walk home the sun was beginning to set.

22. Joggers began to run Sandra smiled at several of them.

23. It was getting dark there were many people in the park.

24. Sandra picked up a pine cone it was lying on the path.

25. Sandra decided to keep the pine cone it reminded her of her new friend.

Extra Practice

Nouns

A. Write whether each underlined noun is a person, place, thing, or idea.

1. Soccer is a rewarding sport.
2. Many people explore the wilderness on foot.
3. Hikers need to think about food, clothing, and shelter.
4. Equipment has to be carried in a backpack.
5. Tents work well for lightweight shelter.
6. The weather can change quickly, so hikers must be prepared.
7. Mountain storms can be fierce, bringing rain, snow, and hail.
8. Without warm, dry clothes, sightseers can be in great danger.
9. Good boots help make any hike a pleasure.
10. Thick socks are important for your comfort.

B. Write each sentence. Draw one line under the noun or nouns in each sentence.

11. The Hamiltons spend much time in the outdoors.
12. Dad spends days on plans for trips to the mountains.
13. Mom fills the backpacks with clothes and food.
14. Ryan carries one tent, and Caitlin carries some pots and pans.
15. Uncle Greg carries the stove and some fuel bottles.
16. Grandma carries a rope and the water bottles.
17. The excited campers cross the narrow bridge above the winding river.
18. Sometimes the adults climb up on glaciers.
19. Both parents have taught people climbing skills.
20. When the family goes to the mountains, every member has a feeling of freedom.

C. Write each sentence. Draw a line under each noun. Then write whether the noun names a person, place, thing, or idea.

21. A person needs common sense in the wilderness.
22. Hikers face many hardships.
23. Animals and the weather can cause trouble.
24. Wild creatures have the right to live in a natural environment.
25. Campers must keep bears out of garbage and stored food.

Singular and Plural Nouns

A. **Write the singular and plural nouns in each sentence.**

1. The sixth-grade class wants to earn money for a class trip.

2. The students hope to earn five hundred dollars.

3. Naoko and her friends want to make and sell birdhouses.

4. She has wood and tools at her house.

5. They make simple boxes out of the wood.

6. Jeremy and Marko use a drill to make holes.

7. Jorge and Leila use nails to put the boards together.

8. It is a good thing there are two workbenches in the shop.

9. The sixth grade made fifteen birdhouses in one day.

10. The houses are finished a week before the holidays begin.

B. **Write the plural form of each underlined noun.**

11. Tomas wants his <u>classmate</u> to earn money for the <u>trip</u>.

12. He wants his <u>friend</u> to suggest the best <u>idea</u> for making money.

13. Their <u>hobby</u> could turn into the best money-making <u>opportunity</u>.

14. Serena makes the birthday <u>card</u> and <u>envelope</u> on her computer.

15. Miguel paints the <u>picture</u> of the <u>baby</u>.

16. Anna makes the <u>toy</u> out of recycled <u>material</u>.

17. She makes the toy <u>boat</u> and <u>bus</u> out of junk.

18. She uses <u>rag</u> to make the stuffed <u>animal</u>.

19. She makes the cutest <u>fox</u> and <u>monkey</u> with button <u>eye</u>.

20. The <u>class</u> will make a great deal of money selling the <u>thing</u>.

C. **Write each sentence. Use the plural form of the noun in parentheses ( ).**

21. The students plan for the fair during math _____. (class)

22. They get a little help from their _____. (teacher)

23. Even their _____ are helping them with plans. (family)

24. Some students will shop at the fair for _____. (present)

25. Naoko and her friends hope the _____ are clear on the day of the fair. (sky)

Extra Practice

More Plural Nouns

A. Write each sentence. Then write *singular* if the underlined noun is singular. Write *plural* if it is plural.

1. Some <u>people</u> study where plants first grew.

2. <u>Tomatoes</u> developed first in the Western Hemisphere.

3. Another food originating there is the <u>potato</u>.

4. Corn, beans, and squash helped feed hungry <u>children</u>.

5. Now <u>chefs</u> all over the world use common American vegetables.

6. Animals such as <u>moose</u> lived only in the Americas.

7. <u>Elk</u> and buffalo wandered in huge herds across the plains.

8. I once saw a <u>buffalo</u> in Yellowstone National Park.

9. Some animals, like <u>mice</u>, are everywhere.

10. I wonder if anyone knows where <u>mosquitoes</u> first developed.

B. Write the plural form of each word below.

11. man

12. leaf

13. chef

14. studio

15. woman

16. elf

17. ox

18. mosquito

19. mouse

20. trout

C. Write each sentence. Write the plural of each noun in parentheses ( ).

21. I wish I could watch _____ of what animal life was like years ago. (video)

22. Rivers were full of _____ swimming upstream. (salmon)

23. _____, bears, and mountain lions lived in the woods. (Wolf)

24. In the autumn, the skies were full of _____ flying south. (goose)

25. There were places so wild that only _____ talk back to you. (echo)

Common and Proper Nouns

A. Write the common nouns in the sentences.

1. Antarctica is the fifth-largest continent.

2. This huge area is also known as the South Pole.

3. Geologists and other scientists do research there.

4. Vincent Massif is the name of the highest point.

5. Penguins live and breed in the icy environment.

6. Many explorers made the South Pole a goal.

7. The first person to succeed was Roald Amundsen.

8. His party arrived on December 14, 1911.

9. A month later, Robert Scott also reached the same part of the continent.

10. No member of that expedition survived the trip home.

B. Write the noun or nouns that should be capitalized in each sentence.

11. Sometimes called rivers of ice, the glaciers of antarctica are beautiful.

12. Many glaciers pour into ross sea.

13. The mackay glacier drops icebergs into the sea.

14. There are many volcanoes to be found on the antarctic peninsula.

15. Students at jefferson elementary school studied the climate there.

16. The world's lowest temperature was taken at vostok station.

17. The coldest months are july and august.

18. In the southern hemisphere, summer is in december.

19. The united states and other nations do research there.

20. The antarctic treaty helps many countries cooperate.

C. Write each sentence. Use capital letters for the proper nouns. Draw a line under each common noun.

21. Many animals live in mcMurdo sound.

22. A source of food for whales, fish, and birds is krill.

23. One student of the tiny, shrimplike animals was dr. reed.

24. This scientist once saw a seal on turtle rock.

25. dr. reed has made several dives in the arctic ocean.

Extra Practice

Capitalization

A. Write and capitalize the underlined proper nouns in these sentences.

1. <u>niki</u> decided to start a club for inventors.

2. She called it the <u>greenwood club</u>.

3. She named it after the inventor <u>chester greenwood</u>.

4. He lived in <u>farmington, maine</u>, where it was often cold.

5. One <u>december</u>, he invented earmuffs.

6. The club met every <u>thursday</u> at 3:30.

7. They discussed inventors, such as <u>carver</u> and <u>curie</u>.

8. They talked about things like the stove invented by <u>franklin</u>.

9. They visited the <u>portland museum</u>.

10. In <u>october</u>, they started working on their own inventions.

B. Write each sentence. Circle each word that needs a capital letter.

11. The club decided that february would be a special month.

12. They named it ancient inventions month.

13. They researched special inventions from asia.

14. I know that jasmine studied early agriculture.

15. She saw an exhibit of farm tools in the smithsonian museum.

16. Such tools were used first in the near east.

17. Another club member, kayi, wondered if paper was invented in china.

18. Inventors in the middle ages designed parachutes.

19. My partner, mario, didn't want to study famous inventions.

20. He wondered if betsy ross invented chocolate chip cookies.

C. Write each sentence with the correct capitalization.

21. amit brought in a special guest on april fools' day.

22. His uncle, mr. khetan, worked at gerstle laboratory.

23. He showed a movie called "try, try again."

24. Even thomas edison had many failures.

25. This news made grady and yan feel better.

Possessive Nouns

A. **Write the possessive noun in each sentence. Write *singular* if the possessive noun is singular and *plural* if it is plural.**

1. Molly's grandmother gave her a camera.

2. The camera's bag had lenses and filters in it.

3. She found photography books in her grandmother's library.

4. The books' photos were outstanding.

5. Ansel Adams's pictures of Yosemite were lovely.

6. Molly liked the animals' pictures best.

7. There was a photo of a deer's antler.

8. The photo showed butterflies' brilliant colors.

9. Her favorite picture froze a hummingbird's flight.

10. Molly couldn't believe the photos' clarity.

B. **Write each sentence. Use the possessive form of the word in parentheses ( ).**

11. Molly took her first roll of film to the _____ counter. (drugstore)

12. She asked for her photography _____ advice. (teacher)

13. Many things affect a _____ quality. (picture)

14. It is important to check a _____ speed. (film)

15. The _____ surface should always be kept clean. (lens)

16. _____ vision is important. (Photographers)

17. Molly asked for her _____ suggestions for subjects. (friends)

18. Close-ups of _____ eyes would be interesting. (insects)

19. Raquel loved to look at _____ faces. (people)

20. Paolo was interested in shooting a _____ flight. (baseball)

C. **Rewrite each phrase to use the possessive form of each underlined noun.**

21. the park of the <u>city</u>

22. the shadows of the <u>gate</u>

23. the flight of the <u>ducks</u>

24. the baseball team of her <u>brothers</u>

25. the face of a <u>baby</u>

Extra Practice

Appositives

A. **Write the appositive in each sentence.**

1. Two climbers, a man and woman from Germany, discovered the Iceman.

2. They found him in the Alps, a mountain range.

3. His location, a distant glacier, was hard to reach.

4. Strange tools, a bow and knife, were beside him.

5. It took time, two days or more, before the world noticed.

6. Rainer Henn, an expert, was called to the site.

7. Bad weather, thick fog, made recovery difficult.

8. Some hay, the lining of his shoes, was still dry.

9. His clothes, finely stitched leather, were lined with fur.

10. The Iceman, an unknown human, will teach us about the past.

B. **Write the appositive. Then write the noun to which it refers.**

11. The Iceman, a middle-aged male, was about 30 years old.

12. A glacier, a thick river of ice, preserved his body.

13. This hunter, a brave man, tells us about life in the Bronze Age.

14. He had good teeth, a full set.

15. Good supplies, warm clothing and protection, were important.

16. He carried a quiver, a pouch for arrows.

17. Tools then were made of bronze, a mixture of copper and tin.

18. His house, one room with a fireplace, was covered with branches.

19. People of the Bronze Age hunted for their food, deer and pigs.

20. They baked loaves of ground-up grains, a kind of coarse flour.

C. **Combine the sentences by forming an appositive.**

21. Many people are studying the Iceman. They are scientists and students.

22. Two countries claimed the Iceman. They are Italy and Austria.

23. The Alps separate Italy from Austria. The Alps are the mountains where the Iceman was found.

24. No one owns the Iceman. He is a messenger from long ago.

25. The Iceman can solve mysteries. He is a symbol of the past.

Combining Sentences: Nouns

A. Write the compound subject or object in each sentence.

1. Saturday or Sunday will be the day of the kite-flying contest.

2. Parents and teachers helped make the kites.

3. Balsa and bamboo are light woods used for kites.

4. Rice paper or cloth will work for kites.

5. A reel or drum holds the string.

6. Aaron and Mei have diamond kites.

7. More people fly box kites and bird kites.

8. Kaori and Leif made their own kites.

9. Dragons or fish were painted on some kites.

10. Children and adults loved watching the kites.

B. Write each pair of sentences as one sentence by combining the subjects or objects with *and* or *or*.

11. The Koreans have flown kites for centuries. The Japanese have flown kites for centuries.

12. Ben Franklin used kites for experiments. Other scientists used kites for experiments.

13. A gust can bring down a kite. A storm can bring down a kite.

14. The weather was perfect. The field was perfect.

15. Mario lost his kite. Mario lost his paper airplane.

16. Trees snagged some strings. Bushes snagged some strings.

17. Kaori kept the kite flying for hours. Logan kept the kite flying for hours.

18. The children held yo-yo contests. They also held bike races.

19. Clowns juggled balls. They also juggled rings.

20. Kites are fun to fly. Paper airplanes are fun to fly.

C. Create a sentence with a compound subject or object, using the sentence given and one of your own.

21. I have a dragon kite.

22. April is a perfect month for flying kites.

23. The park is a safe place to play.

24. You can use paste to attach the paper to the frame.

25. Mei is going to fly her kite tomorrow.

Extra Practice

Action Verbs

A. **Write each action verb. The subject of each sentence has been underlined for you.**

1. The Middletown Fair opens today.

2. I bought five tickets.

3. Lupe asked her mother if she could go.

4. The Ferris wheel towers over the fairgrounds.

5. My friends and I love the fair!

6. Last summer, I earned some spending money by baby-sitting.

7. My friends hugged me because they were happy to go.

8. My mother packed a picnic lunch for us.

9. Our group took the bus to the fairgrounds.

10. We told everyone about the fair.

B. **Write each sentence. Draw a line under each action verb.**

11. The sixth-graders went to Washington, D.C.

12. Our class toured Gettysburg on the way there.

13. In Washington, we visited the Lincoln Memorial first.

14. Then the tour bus brought us to the Capitol.

15. We passed the map back and forth.

16. The whole class enjoyed the White House.

17. Our teacher explained the history of this great building.

18. The President talked to us briefly.

19. Everyone snapped pictures of the President.

20. All of us wrote about the trip on postcards.

C. **Write each sentence using an action verb from the list.**

spoke	won	came	annoyed	created

21. The sixth-graders _____ a mural about Washington, D.C.

22. The mural _____ first prize in the art contest.

23. The principal proudly _____ about our achievement.

24. Some of the winners _____ me with their bickering.

25. Our parents _____ to the award ceremony.

Direct and Indirect Objects

A. Write whether the underlined words are direct objects or indirect objects.

1. Last summer, my family and I rode a <u>bus</u>.
2. We bought my <u>grandmother</u> a <u>ticket</u>, too.
3. Soon enough, we saw <u>Lake Huron</u>.
4. My father splashed <u>water</u> on me.
5. I showed my <u>sister</u> a <u>flock</u> of birds.
6. My sister watched the <u>children</u> build a sand sculpture.
7. We asked the <u>lifeguard</u> a <u>question</u>.
8. My grandmother served <u>us</u> our <u>lunch</u>.
9. On our trip to Lake Huron, we rode <u>bicycles</u> through the trees.
10. In the afternoon, we visited a <u>museum</u>.

B. Write each sentence. Draw one line under the verb. Write *DO* above the direct object and *IO* above the indirect object.

11. My brothers and I sent our grandparents a gift.
12. Mom gave her parents a call.
13. Dad wired Abuela and Abuelo the money for the trip.
14. Abuela and Abuelo wrote my brothers and me a letter.
15. I showed Mom and Dad the note about their trip to Houston.
16. Our friends gave my family a party.
17. The waiters served the diners a wonderful feast.
18. Abuela told her friends a story.
19. Abuelo showed my uncle our pictures.
20. They brought their grandchildren souvenirs from Houston.

C. Write each sentence. Add a direct or an indirect object. Draw one line under each direct object. Draw two lines under each indirect object.

21. Mr. Vasquez earned a _____.
22. His boss gave the _____ a raise.
23. He bought his _____ a new car.
24. Mr. Vasquez showed us an interesting _____ of his car.
25. The car uses _____.

Grammar

Verb Tenses

A. Write *present*, *past*, or *future* to show the tense of each underlined verb.

1. Our principal <u>ordered</u> a computer for every classroom.
2. The whole school <u>raised</u> money for the new computers.
3. Our class <u>washed</u> cars.
4. We also <u>organized</u> a rummage sale.
5. The school <u>will need</u> more money next year.
6. Paper and ink cartridges <u>require</u> more money.
7. Sixth-graders <u>will collect</u> quarters after lunch.
8. Our computer <u>will change</u> the way we learn in school.
9. I <u>announce</u> our project to everyone.
10. I <u>love</u> technology.

B. Write each sentence. Draw one line under the verb. Write whether the verb is in the present, past, or future tense.

11. I enjoy an exciting game.
12. Once I invented an effective mousetrap.
13. My new mousetrap trapped mice really well.
14. My mother hated the mice in the house.
15. I will improve my methods.
16. My next invention thrills my mother.
17. I supplied my mom with a self-cleaning sponge.
18. The invention weighs seventeen pounds.
19. My sister looked at my invention with envy.
20. I will make a million dollars with this invention.

C. Write each sentence. Change each underlined verb to the tense indicated in parentheses.

21. The invention I <u>enjoyed</u> most is the television. (present)
22. I practically <u>live</u> at the swimming pool all summer. (past)
23. My father <u>yells</u> if I watch too much television. (future)
24. I <u>ask</u> my father to join me. (past)
25. My father <u>said</u> he might go swimming with me. (present)

Subject-Verb Agreement

A. Write *yes* if the verb in parentheses agrees with the underlined subject, *no* if it does not.

1. My <u>family</u> (own) a large working farm.

2. <u>We</u> (grows) corn, beans, and squash.

3. In the fall, <u>my dad and I</u> (makes) a maze in the cornfield.

4. <u>He</u> (sells) tickets to enter the maze.

5. <u>I</u> (helps) people go through the maze.

6. The whole <u>town</u> (loves) the maze.

7. <u>People</u> (buys) their pumpkins and squash afterwards.

8. This year my <u>sisters</u> (watches) the action.

9. <u>They</u> (enjoy) the crowds.

10. My <u>dog</u> (likes) the people too.

B. Write each sentence. Complete the sentence with the verb in parentheses that agrees with the subject.

11. Life on a farm (involve, involves) hard work.

12. I (know, knows) that farm life is a great deal of fun.

13. We (raise, raises) pigs and cattle.

14. Cattle (eat, eats) more than pigs.

15. Our baby piglets (keep, keeps) themselves clean.

16. Kyle and I (feed, feeds) the pigs at noon and at five.

17. Children (visit, visits) our farm on field trips.

18. My mother (provide, provides) the snacks.

19. Sometimes my brother (perform, performs) magic tricks.

20. The boys (complete, completes) their chores after dinner.

C. Rewrite each sentence, changing plural subjects to singular subjects. Change the verb so that it agrees with the subject.

21. Our neighbors enjoy visiting Italy.

22. Their relatives live in Rome.

23. The boys write to their family often.

24. Tourists find Italy very romantic.

25. The chefs make excellent pizza.

Grammar

Main Verbs and Helping Verbs

A. Write the helping verb in each underlined verb phrase.

1. We <u>were looking</u> for some fun.

2. The family <u>will prepare</u> a barbecue.

3. My sister <u>can make</u> her famous pasta salad.

4. Mom <u>has been getting</u> ready for weeks.

5. Jenna <u>might bring</u> the chips and dip.

6. Mario <u>is buying</u> the hamburger meat.

7. I <u>have checked</u> the barbecue grill.

8. Who <u>would like</u> to light the charcoal?

9. My father <u>might be</u> willing to help.

10. Dad <u>has helped</u> in the past.

B. Write the sentence. Underline the verb phrase. Circle the helping verb.

11. Many events should be planned for Founder's Day.

12. Next year I may invite my relatives from overseas.

13. I shall write a letter inviting them.

14. You would enjoy this celebration.

15. They were hoping for a game of volleyball.

16. Parades, concerts, and fireworks will be held during the event.

17. My brother might play in the band.

18. Sharon could perform one of her dances.

19. We will need some money.

20. The Founder's Day party can cost a lot of money.

C. Write each sentence. Complete the sentence by using the correct helping verb in parentheses.

21. The day of the party (are, will) arrive sooner than we think.

22. Carina (has, did) decided to participate in the croquet tournament.

23. Emmie and Annie (were, can) help set up the pins for lawn bowling.

24. The boys (does, do) not need to work so hard.

25. We (have, has) always held a celebration in September.

Commas

A. **Write each sentence. Place a comma or commas where needed in each underlined group of words.**

1. I was born on <u>December 17 1980</u>.

2. Our first house was in <u>Marvella Texas</u>.

3. <u>We did however move</u> shortly after I was born.

4. <u>Yes that was difficult</u> for my mother.

5. She had to choose <u>a house a mover, and a painter</u>.

6. <u>My cat Stella almost got lost</u> in the move.

7. <u>My father the hero,</u> eventually found her.

8. Our next house was in <u>Topeka Kansas</u>.

9. <u>Please let's not</u> move again.

10. <u>Simon please help</u> Mom unpack those boxes.

B. **Write each sentence. Put in the missing commas.**

11. You can see the Liberty Bell in Philadelphia Pennsylvania.

12. We went to see the bell on Tuesday July 5.

13. There is no charge of course to see the Liberty Bell.

14. Yes the Liberty Bell is cracked.

15. Sure there are other things to see in Philadelphia.

16. There is an art museum a science museum and beautiful parks.

17. Mom and Dad you might consider taking us to Philadelphia.

18. We could go on from there to Washington D.C.

19. Yes that would that be fantastic!

20. Let's plan this trip for June 10 2012.

C. **Rewrite the sentences. Add the phrase in parentheses to each sentence. Use commas to set off the added text.**

21. My cousin is going to Hawaii. (a sixth-grade teacher)

22. She is talented with pencils. (watercolors and charcoals)

23. Hawaii will inspire my cousin to paint. (a beautiful place)

24. Everyone says Teah is talented. (including her art teacher)

25. Teah plans to study at the Art Institute. (a well-known school in Chicago)

Extra Practice

Progressive Forms

A. Write whether the underlined verb phrase is present progressive or past progressive.

1. Today our town <u>is holding</u> a Clean-Up Day.

2. All families <u>are participating</u> this year.

3. Some children <u>were picking</u> up litter earlier.

4. Some people <u>were working</u> to clean up the river banks.

5. These days our trash <u>is cluttering</u> the river banks.

6. The boys and girls <u>are doing</u> an excellent job right now.

7. At this time, the city sewers <u>are filling</u> up with trash.

8. The street workers <u>were trying</u> to clean the drainage ditches.

9. For years, we <u>were neglecting</u> the natural beauty of our parks.

10. Now we <u>are taking</u> good care of our parks.

B. Write each sentence. Choose the correct form of the helping verb in parentheses.

11. Tonight, the mayor (is, was) deciding what to do about litter.

12. Last week, everyone (is, was) calling the mayor to complain.

13. The children (are, is) organizing a task force now.

14. All last week, the street cleaners (were, are) working hard.

15. A month ago, some of the sewers (were, are) overflowing.

16. Now the sewers (were, are) no longer backing up.

17. The whole town (is, was) beginning to look beautiful.

18. Businesses along Main Street (is, are) providing trash barrels.

19. Students (is, are) making posters about the cleanup effort.

20. I (am, are) writing to the newspapers about our newly cleaned town.

C. Write each sentence. Use the present-progressive or the past-progressive form of the verb in parentheses.

21. I _____ to clean my room today. (go)

22. The children _____ hard all last week for their math test. (study)

23. Two years ago, my neighbors _____ in Pittsburgh, PA. (live)

24. Now my best friend, Aaron, _____ right next door. (live)

25. My sister _____ for her doll in the closet for three hours. (look)

Perfect Tenses

A. **Write whether the underlined verb phrase is present perfect or past perfect.**

1. We <u>have learned</u> new facts and skills in language arts.

2. Before this school year, we <u>had studied</u> spelling.

3. We <u>have studied</u> verb tenses this entire week.

4. We <u>had worked</u> with commas for a day before I understood them.

5. Previously, I <u>had thought</u> that semicolons were dull.

6. I <u>had spent</u> a month on quotation marks before they made sense.

7. I <u>have attended</u> Jefferson Elementary School for six years.

8. Our class <u>had tried</u> to do a project alone until we asked for help.

9. I <u>have tried</u> to memorize a grammar rule each day.

10. Before Juan passed the test, he <u>had studied</u> for two weeks.

B. **Write each sentence. Choose the correct verb in parentheses.**

11. I (have read, has read) some books by Robert Louis Stevenson.

12. Until recently, she (have written, had written) only one paper.

13. By 6:00 P.M., I (had finished, has finished) my homework.

14. Everyone (has tried, have tried) a few interesting experiences.

15. Reporters (has written, have written) about what they know.

16. Children (has memorized, have memorized) punctuation rules.

17. By 8:00, the baby (had slept, have slept) for two hours already.

18. I wrote my essay after I (has found, had found) all the facts.

19. You (have passed, has passed) the test with a good score.

20. Before I started my essay, I (has not known, had not known) how much fun it could be to write.

C. **Write each sentence. Use the present-perfect or past-perfect tense of the verb in parentheses.**

21. Some children _____ that school can be fun. (realize)

22. They _____ a great effort this year. (made)

23. Kareem _____ hard, and now his essay was done. (work)

24. Miss Jones _____ the class about the test every day. (remind)

25. Last month, the class _____ often to prepare themselves. (study)

203

Extra Practice

Linking Verbs

A. Write the linking verb in each sentence. The predicate nouns and predicate adjectives are identified.

1. I am Jess. *(PN)*

2. I feel sick today. *(PA)*

3. I stayed quiet all day, but it didn't help. *(PA)*

4. Now it is midnight. *(PN)*

5. I seem worse when I look out the window. *(PA)*

6. My mother was my nurse. *(PN)*

7. "You appear fine," she said. *(PA)*

8. My complexion looks flushed. *(PA)*

9. I became well by the end of the day. *(PA)*

10. I felt fine all of a sudden! *(PA)*

B. Write each sentence. Circle the linking verb and draw one line under the predicate noun or the predicate adjective.

11. This dance is quite important to me.

12. My group is enthusiastic about learning a new routine.

13. They feel curious about a different style of dance.

14. Some dancers seem nervous about the instructor.

15. However, I am calm.

16. My friends and I can be good dancers if we practice.

17. My older brother is a dancer.

18. He appears very skilled at dancing.

19. A good dancer becomes another character when performing.

20. This new dancer looks graceful.

C. Write the sentences. Complete each sentence with a linking verb. Then draw one line under the word that identifies or describes the subject.

21. The Rosa Parks Elementary School dance _____ fantastic.

22. Everyone _____ excited that the dance was a sock-hop.

23. The students _____ terrific in their good clothes.

24. The refreshments _____ delicious and everyone ate them.

25. Everyone _____ sad when the dance ended.

Irregular Verbs

A. **Write the irregular verb in each sentence.**

1. We went on a great vacation.

2. We flew to Louisiana.

3. Then we drove to the coast.

4. I had done this trip before.

5. My brother and I rode in the back seat.

6. He took drawing paper and pens with him.

7. We drew pictures of the faces of people around us.

8. I knew all the people in my brother's pictures.

9. Then we wrote stories about these people.

10. I saw some interesting sights along the way, too.

B. **Write each sentence. Choose the correct verb in parentheses to complete the sentence.**

11. I have (took, taken) plenty of trips with my family.

12. We've (driven, drove) through thirteen different states.

13. We (flown, flew) across the country, but that was expensive.

14. We (seen, saw) the most amazing sights from the airplane.

15. When we landed, we (gone, went) straight to the motel.

16. My mother (knew, known) we would want to rest.

17. My family has (did, done) a lot of work to get here.

18. We (took, taken) hikes, camped, and fished.

19. I have (knew, known) people who really enjoyed mountain trips.

20. My friend, Tato, (written, wrote) about his trip in his journal.

C. **Write the sentences. Use the correct form of the verb in parentheses to complete each sentence.**

21. We have _____ a list of new ideas. (write)

22. Yesterday, LeeAnn _____ nothing about this list. (know)

23. My mother _____ a look at the new list. (take)

24. Afterwards she _____ we were on the right track. (see)

25. Why _____ this seem so difficult? (do)

Extra Practice

Personal Pronouns: Singular and Plural

A. Write whether the underlined personal pronoun in each sentence is singular or plural.

1. <u>She</u> wants to enter the art contest.

2. <u>We</u> will help gather materials for a sculpture.

3. Rosa, will <u>you</u> work with clay, cardboard, paints, or paper?

4. <u>He</u> will be the instructor.

5. The assistant will teach <u>us</u> to paint.

6. That long brush is for <u>me</u>.

7. <u>I</u> am nervous about displaying my work.

8. Paco and Dee, <u>you</u> will have no problem after the lesson.

9. <u>We</u> entered the studio and began to listen.

10. <u>It</u> was the most exciting experience.

B. Write the sentences. Circle each personal pronoun.

11. Alicia painted with me.

12. Stephan brought his own paints with him.

13. A group of friends saw them in the studio.

14. I would love to attend this class again.

15. We all painted bright, detailed pictures.

16. Can he give another art lesson soon?

17. The friends were so proud of us.

18. They will all help clean up the room.

19. I hope to bring Omar next time.

20. Did you see the finished paintings?

C. Write each sentence. Replace the underlined proper or common noun(s) with a personal pronoun.

21. <u>Curtis, Alicia, and Stephan</u> planned to sketch a mural.

22. <u>Curtis</u> drew a picture first.

23. The teacher told <u>Alicia and me</u> to draw something next.

24. <u>Alicia and I</u> added a park scene.

25. Painting and sketching was fun for <u>Curtis</u>.

Pronouns and Referents

A. **Read each sentence. Then write the pronoun and its referent.**

1. Susie researched her report on Egypt.

2. The Internet was helpful because it provided information.

3. Roberto shared his computer with Susie.

4. Susie and Roberto worked hard on their project.

5. Susie searched the Web site to find her information.

6. Roberto had a turn, and he found a picture of a pyramid.

7. Susie and Roberto realized they could help each other.

8. The teacher said she was pleased.

9. Did Sharifa save the information on her disk?

10. The information will be useful when I need it.

B. **Write each sentence. Use the correct pronouns in parentheses.**
Select the pronoun that matches the underlined referent.

11. Roberto helped Susie, and (she, he) helped Roberto.

12. Roberto and Susie used (their, our) information to write a paper.

13. Roberto said (he, him) was happy with what he found.

14. The scanner was needed, but (they, it) wasn't available.

15. I liked working with Susie, and she liked working with (her, me).

16. The teacher sent us to the library to begin writing (our, your)
research paper.

17. "If (she, I) can help you, please let me know."

18. The teacher talked to Susie about (my, her) question about Egypt.

19. The students worked hard when (they, them) had an assignment.

20. We use encyclopedias because (it, they) contain good information.

C. **Write each sentence. Write a pronoun in each**
blank that matches the underlined referent.

21. Roberto and I created a pyramid for _____ project.

22. Susie took great pride in _____ project.

23. The students watched a video that taught
_____ how an archeologist digs for artifacts.

24. Roberto presented _____ project next.

25. Roberto and Susie placed _____ projects on the table.

Extra Practice

Subject and Object Pronouns

A. Write the personal pronoun in each sentence. Tell whether the word is a subject pronoun or an object pronoun.

1. Are you going fishing this weekend?

2. Dad helped me with the equipment.

3. Sam took a fishing hat and put it on his head.

4. He was excited about the fishing trip.

5. They packed the car and were ready to leave.

6. The family took a fishing boat, and the car pulled it.

7. They planned to fish for five days.

8. Sam brought his tackle box and carried it with his gear.

9. The map guided them to the cabin.

10. They arrived and unpacked the car.

B. Write each sentence. Write *S* above each subject pronoun and *O* above each object pronoun. Write the referent for each pronoun.

11. Dad and Jeff wanted an early start, so they went to bed early.

12. Dad asked the cabin owner to give him a wake-up call.

13. The gear was packed, so Dad put it into the boat.

14. The boat landing was old, and it was rickety.

15. Dad called, "Help me, son!"

16. Dad hitched the boat and trailer and backed them down to the water's edge.

17. When Dad unhitched the boat, it slid easily into the lake.

18. Jeff held out a worm, and Dad put it on a hook.

19. When family members caught fish, they threw them back into the lake.

20. It was an exciting fishing trip!

C. Write each sentence. Choose a pronoun to fill in the blank.

21. The fisherman didn't move as _____ watched the water.

22. He said, "_____ am glad the fish are biting today, aren't you?"

23. The men caught fish and cooked _____ in a pan.

24. Sam grabbed his net and shook the water out of _____.

25. The men had fun because _____ caught large fish all day.

Combining Sentences: Subject and Object Pronouns

A. Underline the compound subject or compound object in each sentence.

1. Gretta and I wanted to go to the park.

2. Sauki and she took skates to the park.

3. Leila invited Joseph and me to go.

4. He and his friends packed a picnic lunch.

5. Joseph served Leila and me.

6. Gretta and she provided the drinks.

7. Sauki and I had knee pads and a helmet for skating.

8. Joseph had a picnic and cookout with Gretta and her.

9. He and Ralph skated on the path and basketball court.

10. Gretta and he ate the brownies.

B. Write each sentence. Use the correct word in parentheses.

11. Ralph and (she, her) tripped and fell.

12. Leila and (I, me) enjoyed the picnic.

13. The food satisfied my friends and (I, me).

14. Joseph and (she, her) ate potato chips.

15. The jogger helped Ralph and (they, you).

16. Sauki and (he, him) took a break from skating.

17. Leila gave some soda to Joseph and (she, her).

18. Ralph invited a younger boy and (I, me) to rest on a bench.

19. Joseph and (she, her) began picking up the picnic.

20. Ralph and (I, me) put on protective gear again.

C. Combine each pair of sentences by forming compound subjects or compound objects. Write the new sentence.

21. After the picnic, she picked up the trash. I also picked up the trash.

22. Sauki skated home. He skated home.

23. Sauki greeted him. She greeted her friends.

24. He gathered the food. Leila gathered the food.

25. Gretta helped Leila load the car. Gretta helped him load the car.

Extra Practice

Punctuation in Dialogue

A. Write the sentences. Draw a line under the name of the person who is speaking in each sentence. Circle the quotation marks.

1. Patty asked, "Do you want to go to the movies with us?"

2. "We would love to go," said Oliver.

3. "What day is best for you?" asked Patty.

4. Angela responded, "Wednesday is good."

5. "Great!" exclaimed Alex.

6. "Good," replied Patty. "Wednesday works for me, too."

7. "I haven't been to that theater," said Alex.

8. "It's cool," commented Omar. "They have huge screens."

9. "I have only been to that theater once," added Angela.

10. "How much money should we bring?" questioned Alex.

B. Write each sentence correctly. Draw one line under the direct quotation.

11. "I think," said Omar, "that you should wear long pants."

12. "Is the theater cold?" asked Alex.

13. "Who will be taking us?" asked Hector.

14. "My mom will drive," responded Patty.

15. "I can't wait!" yelled Angela.

16. Alex commented, "Let's get pizza after the movie."

17. "Alex," responded Omar, "that's a great idea."

18. Patty said, "We'll go to Pizza Palace on Elm Avenue."

19. "Have you eaten there before?" questioned Angela.

20. "Yes, the pizza is delicious, and there's a game room in the back," replied Patty.

C. Write each sentence correctly. Add quotation marks, capital letters, commas, and end punctuation when necessary.

21. I had a great time last Saturday said Alex.

22. that movie was so funny, remarked Omar.

23. The pizza was divine exclaimed Angela.

24. Patty asked should we try to get together every Saturday

25. Yes said the others, we'd love to!

Indefinite Pronouns

A. Write whether the underlined indefinite pronoun in each sentence is singular or plural.

1. The team had extra tickets and gave <u>several</u> to their friends.

2. <u>Everyone</u> will be able to go.

3. "<u>Each</u> should bring a glove."

4. <u>Some</u> took a permanent marker for an autograph.

5. "Did you bring <u>something</u> for a snack?"

6. "I'd give <u>anything</u> for the pitcher's autograph."

7. <u>Both</u> bought a baseball cap at the stadium.

8. <u>Most</u> wore their team shirt to the game.

9. <u>All</u> were excited about being at the game.

10. <u>Nothing</u> was going to spoil their day.

B. Write each sentence. Draw one line under the indefinite pronoun.

11. Someone caught a foul ball.

12. "Did anyone see that play?"

13. Few ordered nachos.

14. Others ordered hot dogs.

15. I don't have any relish. Do you have some?

16. Many stood up during the seventh-inning stretch.

17. "Is there anything left in your cup?"

18. "Did you get something to eat?"

19. Both bought a T-shirt from the ballpark.

20. "Nobody will forget this game."

C. Write each sentence. Fill in the blank with an indefinite pronoun.

21. _____ forgot her program.

22. _____ in the group caught a foul ball.

23. _____ wanted to go home.

24. The game was loved by _____.

25. _____ took pictures during the game.

211

Extra Practice

Pronoun-Verb Agreement

A. **Write each sentence. Draw a line under the subject pronoun and the verb.**

1. She likes swim races.

2. She practices at the local pool with friends.

3. They gather at the pool twice a week.

4. We hope to race in a swim meet soon.

5. They are held at an Olympic-sized pool.

6. I think the swim meets will be tiring.

7. You have to dive into the pool first.

8. She wants to learn to swim fast.

9. I want to swim in the ocean.

10. They haven't tried that yet.

B. **Write each sentence. Choose the verb in parentheses that agrees with the subject pronoun.**

11. They (practice, practices) proper breathing techniques.

12. She (enjoy, enjoys) learning all the techniques.

13. You must (swim, swims) well to win a race.

14. He (was, were) an instructor in my last swim class.

15. It (help, helps) people improve their skills.

16. We (take, takes) tests in order to pass the class.

17. She (has learned, have learned) two new strokes.

18. We (are planning, is planning) a picnic after the first meet.

19. They (have, has) all the details worked out for us.

20. I (are, am) excited about this experience.

C. **Write each sentence. Choose the subject pronoun in the parentheses that agrees with the verb.**

21. (We, I) are in a swim meet this Saturday.

22. (He, They) reminds us of the safety tips.

23. (She, They) stretch and warm up before the meet.

24. (I, He) put on my goggles first.

25. (He, We) swim as fast as we can.

Possessive Pronouns

A. Write the possessive pronoun in each sentence.

1. Molly borrowed her favorite book from the library.

2. The book is not hers, so she handled it carefully.

3. The story is about a farmer and his daughter.

4. Their farm is in trouble because of a terrible drought.

5. The farmer decides to sell some of his equipment.

6. A friend agrees to hold an auction on her property.

7. Suddenly a cow begins shaking its tail.

8. The girl says, "My cow is giving us a signal."

9. "Rain will come to our farm!" exclaimed the father.

10. The farmer and daughter smiled as they canceled their auction.

B. Write the sentences. Use the correct possessive pronoun in parentheses.

11. Frederick selected a book about (our, ours) state.

12. He learned that (him, his) ancestors had settled here.

13. Leaving (they, their) homes in Germany, they had sailed across the ocean.

14. He designed a poster to illustrate (their, they) travels.

15. (Our, Ours) class was interested in his family's history.

16. "(Your, You) family sounds adventurous," said Ross.

17. Sally thinks (hers, her) ancestors are from Norway.

18. She hopes to find a book on (they, their) explorations.

19. Rafe wants to read about the beetle and (it, its) habitat.

20. (Our, Ours) school library has a variety of books.

C. Write each sentence. Add a possessive pronoun to complete it.

21. Mrs. Pitt said, "Those books are _____ favorites."

22. They tell about brave leaders and _____ courageous acts.

23. Put that book in _____ correct place.

24. I already put _____ on the bottom shelf.

25. We enjoy borrowing books from _____ library.

Extra Practice

Adjectives

A. Write the adjective that modifies the underlined nouns.

1. Dinosaurs were extraordinary <u>animals</u>.
2. These extinct <u>animals</u> laid eggs.
3. Dinosaur means "terrible <u>lizard</u>."
4. Unlike lizards, dinosaurs had long <u>legs</u>.
5. Crocodiles are dinosaurs' nearest <u>relatives</u>.
6. Iguanas have sharp <u>claws</u> like dinosaurs.
7. There are scary <u>dinosaurs</u> in the museum!
8. Their immense <u>bodies</u> can fill a room.
9. In 1820, Dr. Gideon Mantell found several <u>teeth</u>.
10. Dr. Mantell concluded that the teeth belonged to a giant <u>reptile</u>.

B. Write each sentence. Circle the adjectives. Draw arrows from the adjectives to the words they modify.

11. Many people think of dinosaurs as massive creatures.
12. There were tiny dinosaurs that wouldn't even reach your knee.
13. Two huge dinosaurs are Brachiosaurus and Supersaurus.
14. My favorite dinosaur is Stegosaurus.
15. Stegosaurus had bony plates along its back.
16. Several dinosaurs had spiked tails.
17. It would be an experience to see any dinosaur!
18. The duck-billed dinosaur had spectacular teeth.
19. Hundreds of sharp, diamond-shaped teeth lined the jaws of some dinosaurs.
20. The dinosaur, fierce and aggressive, gobbled up the plants in its path.

C. Write each sentence. Fill in each blank with an adjective.

21. Some scientists think dinosaurs died from eating _____ plants.
22. Some blame a meteorite for the _____ extinction of dinosaurs.
23. Perhaps the dinosaurs froze to death in an _____ ice age.
24. Some _____ theories about their disappearance have emerged.
25. Will no one solve the _____ mystery of dinosaur extinction?

Articles: *a, an, the*

A. **Write each article and the word that follows it.**

1. Suppose you won a trip to either the Arctic or the Antarctic.

2. Many people think the two places are the same, but they're not.

3. One is the North Pole, and the other is called the South Pole.

4. To see a penguin, you could go to the Antarctic.

5. Will it be a big surprise to find an Arctic bird in Mexico?

6. You can find a swarm of bees in some parts of the Arctic!

7. You might also see a glacier, a mass of slow-moving ice.

8. An iceberg is an enormous block of ice.

9. Icebergs can rise a hundred feet from the ocean's surface.

10. During an Arctic night, the sky often flickers with bright colors.

B. **Write each sentence, using the correct article.**

11. Only about one-eighth of (a, an) iceberg shows above the water.

12. (A, The) largest part of an iceberg is hidden below water.

13. (A, An) ship's captain may not know where an iceberg begins and ends.

14. In 1912, (an, a) "unsinkable" ship sailed from England to New York.

15. (A, The) famous ship, *Titanic*, never arrived in New York.

16. Robert Peary and Matthew Henson were (a, the) first explorers to reach the North Pole.

17. Antarctica is truly (a, the) last frontier.

18. Of all seven continents, Antarctica is (a, the) hardest to reach.

19. No wonder it took (an, a) explorer so long to discover it!

20. Roald Amundsen was (a, the) first explorer to reach Antarctica.

C. **Write the sentences. Fill in the missing articles.**

21. _____ elephant cannot live in Antarctica.

22. Whales swim in _____ ocean, but they are not fish.

23. Arctic hares have _____ coat that changes color with _____ seasons.

24. I saw _____ picture of _____ Arctic fox and _____ polar bear.

25. Arctic birds migrate halfway around _____ world.

Extra Practice

Demonstrative Adjectives

A. Write the demonstrative adjective in each sentence.

1. That oak tree is at the far edge of our property.

2. This apple tree is very close to my house.

3. Look at that giant sequoia.

4. We are amazed at the size of those spruce trees.

5. Mr. Fujita raised these bonsai trees.

6. This palm tree has a rough, scratchy trunk.

7. Let's paint a picture of those pine trees on the mountain.

8. Why is that elm tree losing all its leaves?

9. Mom told us to rake these leaves before we go to the mall.

10. José plans to use this red leaf for his collection.

B. Write each sentence, using the correct demonstrative adjective.

11. (That, Those) palm tree does not have any branches.

12. (This, Those) trees produce dates and coconuts.

13. Please come and take a look at (that, this) unusual fern.

14. A new tree will grow from (these, this) seed.

15. (That, This) ginkgo looks tiny because it is so far away.

16. (These, This) cedar trees need to be planted over there.

17. Many bushels of apples are produced in (those, that) orchard.

18. Come over and have a peach from (that, this) tree in my yard.

19. (That, Those) medicine comes from a tree that grows in South America.

20. (These, This) syrup comes from maple trees.

C. Write each sentence. Fill in the demonstrative adjective.

21. The koala bears here in the zoo eat nothing but the leaves of _____ eucalyptus trees.

22. _____ tree frog on the highest branch has suction pads on its feet.

23. Can you see _____ caterpillars over there eating the leaves?

24. I found _____ ladybug in my backyard.

25. _____ forest fire last year destroyed thousands of acres.

Proper Adjectives

A. Write the proper adjective in each sentence.

1. This store has food from all over the world, including Irish cheese.

2. Look at the squares of Turkish taffy.

3. My father likes British pudding.

4. We bought a pound of Israeli oranges.

5. The warm French bread smells delicious.

6. I use Italian olive oil on my salad.

7. My grandmother likes Polish sausage.

8. African peanuts are good in stew.

9. Egyptian dates and figs hang from the ceiling.

10. Do you enjoy German chocolate cake?

B. Rewrite each sentence. Capitalize the proper adjective.

11. Have you tried english muffins for breakfast?

12. The canadian dollar is quite colorful.

13. We bought danish pastry at the deli.

14. The japanese flag has a red circle at its center.

15. Have you ever seen a korean flag?

16. Some people love hot and spicy thai dishes.

17. Once, spanish galleons loaded with gold sailed the seas.

18. Cumin is a spice used in indian dishes.

19. The greek capital is Athens.

20. The Statue of Liberty is the symbol of american freedom.

C. Complete each sentence by forming a proper adjective from the noun in parentheses. Write the sentence.

21. Sean spoke with an _____ accent. (Ireland)

22. Parrots inhabit _____ jungles. (South America)

23. Some _____ natives live high in the Andes Mountains. (Peru)

24. On cold nights we drink _____ hot chocolate. (Mexico)

25. Making and flying box kites are ancient _____ skills. (China)

Extra Practice

Comparative and Superlative Adjectives

A. Write the comparative or superlative adjective in each sentence.

1. The spring fair is the largest event in the city.
2. This year's fair is larger than last year's.
3. Today's weather is nicer than yesterday's.
4. It is warmer than it was last May.
5. Our prizes are bigger than the ones given in the Oldfield carnival.
6. The ring toss is easier than the batting cage.
7. The bumper cars are the fastest I have ever driven!
8. The roller coaster is the busiest ride at the fair.
9. Tim is the shortest player on the Red team.
10. In the broad jump, I jumped a foot higher than last year.
11. In the tug of war, the team with the heavier players won.
12. The man with the stronger arms won the joust.
13. Seth is one of the finest banjo players in the county.
14. The meanest bull at the rodeo threw ten riders.
15. On the midway, people could see the skinniest man in the world.
16. Josh was the strongest person in the weightlifting contest.
17. The balloon pop is the easiest game of all.
18. A baseball game is longer than a soccer match.
19. The latest person to arrive must go to the end of the line.
20. That clown has the saddest face.

B. **Write each sentence. Underline the comparative or superlative adjective. Tell which things are being compared.**

21. The peaches are sweeter than the apples.

22. The watermelon is the largest fruit of all.

23. The rolls are fresher than the bread.

24. Snakes are among the thinnest reptiles on Earth.

25. The fresh peas are healthier than the canned ones.

26. The canned corn is fresher than the frozen kind.

27. The farmer's market is newer than the grocery store.

28. Our school library is the oldest building on campus.

29. The school is prettier than the town hall.

30. That's the saddest song in the music book.

C. **Rewrite the sentences. Change the adjectives in parentheses to their correct comparative or superlative forms.**

31. By day, Mercury is (hot) than Earth.

32. The sun is the (bright) object in our solar system.

33. The moon appears to be the (shiny) object in the night sky.

34. Mercury is the (near) planet to the sun.

35. Jupiter is the (large) planet in our solar system.

36. Venus is (small) than Saturn.

37. The (tiny) planet is Pluto.

38. Jupiter has a (slow) orbit than Mars.

39. Mercury has the (fast) orbit of all—88 Earth days.

40. The moon is not visible on the (dark) night of the year.

Extra Practice

Comparing with *More* and *Most*

A. **Write the comparative or superlative adjectives.**

1. The winters are the most unbearable in the polar regions.

2. The most successful travelers take their video cameras on trips.

3. An ocean liner is more seaworthy than a rubber raft.

4. I think Texas would be more fun to visit than another state.

5. A vacation in the city is more interesting than a trip to the beach.

6. The South Pole is the most frigid place on Earth.

7. I think Nova Scotia is more beautiful than Ontario.

8. Florida has the most wonderful theme parks in America!

9. I think the mountains are more magnificent than the seashore.

10. Some think the Grand Canyon is the most exciting place to visit.

B. **Rewrite each sentence. Use the correct word in parentheses.**

11. Thunderstorms are (more, most) dangerous than regular storms.

12. Hurricanes are the (most, more) hazardous storms of all.

13. The winds are (more, most) intense during a hurricane than they are during a regular storm.

14. The rain may be (most, more) powerful during a tornado than during a thunderstorm.

15. The (most, more) protective place of all during a tornado is a shelter.

16. Hurricanes are (most, more) destructive than other storms.

17. A tsunami is (most, more) violent than a mild seaquake.

18. Lightning is the (most, most) terrifying part of a storm.

19. The (most, more) peaceful part of a storm is the "eye."

20. The (more, most) forceful winds of all are outside the eye.

C. **Write the sentences, using the correct comparative or superlative form of the adjective in parentheses.**

21. Science is the _____ subject. (exciting)

22. Clouds seem _____ than people realize. (important)

23. Sunny days are _____ than stormy days. (pleasurable)

24. Rain is _____ to crops than sunshine is. (vital)

25. Weather is the _____ factor for a farmer. (changeable)

Comparing with *Good* and *Bad*

A. Write the correct comparative or superlative form of *good* or *bad* in each sentence.

1. Apples are (better, best) for you than candy.

2. Soda is the (worst, worse) food of all.

3. It is (better, best) to eat three meals a day.

4. Some snack foods are (worst, worse) than others.

5. The (better, best) thing about fruit is its taste.

6. To me, fruit tastes (better, best) than salty snack foods.

7. Nick thinks broccoli is (worse, worst) than spinach.

8. He thinks eggplant is the (worse, worst) vegetable!

9. Some people think eggplant is (best, better) than cauliflower.

10. The (worst, worse) diet is one made up mostly of "junk" food.

B. Rewrite each sentence, using the correct form of *good* or *bad*.

11. Sammi likes baseball (more better, better) than volleyball.

12. She thinks soccer is the (most best, best) sport of all.

13. Lou says football is the (worst, worser) sport.

14. He argues that football is (worser, worse) than baseball.

15. I think water polo is the (bestest, best) sport in the world!

16. It's (more better, better) to try a new sport than to do nothing.

17. The (best, most good) sports have a lot of action.

18. The (baddest, worst) sports are boring.

19. Some players believe that it's (more bad, worse) to lose by one point than by many points.

20. The (better, best) way to exercise is to have fun at the same time.

C. Write each sentence, using the correct form of the adjective.

21. It's (good) to sleep at least eight hours a night than two hours.

22. My mother says the (bad) thing is not getting enough sleep.

23. Your health will become much (good) after you start exercising.

24. I think it's (bad) to skip meals than to eat snack foods.

25. One of the (bad) things you can do is not to eat right.

Extra Practice

Combining Sentences: Adjectives

A. Write the adjectives that can be joined to combine each pair of sentences.

1. Traveling to famous places is fun. It's educational.

2. Great Salt Lake is unique. Great Salt Lake is interesting.

3. The Humber Bridge in England looks long. It looks sturdy.

4. Stonehenge is large. Stonehenge is mysterious.

5. The Eiffel Tower is beautiful. The Eiffel Tower is majestic.

6. The streets in Florence are narrow. The streets are winding.

7. The Tower of Pisa is tall. The Tower of Pisa is lopsided.

8. Fjords in Norway are long. Fjords in Norway are narrow.

9. The Petrified Forest looks painted. It looks unreal.

10. Angel Falls is a tall waterfall. It's also powerful.

B. Combine each pair of sentences into one new sentence.

11. The Statue of Liberty looks proud. It looks friendly.

12. Yellowstone was America's first national park. It is the largest.

13. Sequoias are the world's oldest trees. They are the largest.

14. The Galápagos Islands have rocky soil. The soil is volcanic, too.

15. Giant tortoises are rare animals. Giant tortoises are massive.

16. Easter Island has mysterious statues. It has ancient statues.

17. Egyptian pyramids are impressive. They are popular.

18. The Sahara is the world's biggest desert. It is the most famous.

19. There are old cliff dwellings at Mesa Verde. They are white.

20. The anxious tourists eagerly entered the gate. They were excited.

C. Write each sentence. Use an adjective from one sentence to combine the two sentences. Underline the adjective you added.

21. The celebrated Taj Mahal was built long ago in India. It is grand.

22. The Taj Mahal has a large white dome. The dome is peaked.

23. For an exciting vacation, visit Australia. Your vacation will be unusual.

24. Ayers Rock is a solitary rock in Australia. It is huge.

25. Ayers Rock is the largest rock in the world. It is the most famous.

Abbreviations

A. Write the word that can be abbreviated.

1. Mister Chin visited Boston on business.

2. In December, the class went to the Everglades.

3. The directions noted a right turn on Smith Street.

4. Doctor Glikos drove to El Paso.

5. We're going to Yosemite in California.

6. Governor Wilson dedicated a statue in Petersburg.

7. The field trip will be to Saguaro, Arizona.

8. On Thursday we packed our bags for a class trip.

9. Senator Peters will go with us on the trip.

10. On the way we will stop in New Mexico.

B. Write the abbreviation for each underlined word.

11. In November we celebrate Thanksgiving.

12. The holiday always falls on the fourth Thursday of the month.

13. Mister Lewis is bringing sweet potatoes to the dinner.

14. My birthday is on January 7.

15. Amy is taking me to see a movie on Tuesday.

16. Her dental appointment is with Doctor Thomas.

17. She lives close by, on Sunset Avenue.

18. The neighbors used to live in New York.

19. Rosa's cousins live at 318 Osler Drive.

20. They live in Parsippany, New Jersey.

C. Write the sentences. Write one word or phrase as an abbreviation.

21. I called my friend who lives on Elm Street.

22. She agreed to meet at the library on First Avenue.

23. We made plans to finish our report by November.

24. Doctor Greenspan agreed to be interviewed by us.

25. Her office is on Brightman Road.

Extra Practice

Adverbs That Modify Verbs

A. **Write the adverb that describes the underlined verb in each sentence.**

1. Brandon excitedly <u>jumped</u> to his feet.

2. He anxiously <u>watched</u> as his brother ran to first base.

3. His brother, David, swiftly <u>rounded</u> first.

4. The first baseman eagerly <u>caught</u> the ball.

5. Hastily, David <u>charged</u> to second base.

6. Kimmy, playing second base, calmly <u>caught</u> the ball.

7. As the crowd <u>cheered</u> mightily, Kimmy tagged David.

8. "Nice play," David <u>sighed</u> politely.

9. "Awesome!" Brandon reassuringly <u>called</u> from the stands.

10. David gratefully <u>waved</u> to his little brother.

B. **Write each sentence. Write _ADV_ above each adverb. Write _V_ above each verb.**

11. Afterward, Brandon and his parents waited for David.

12. The baseball coach was speaking quietly to the team.

13. The boys and girls on the team listened closely.

14. The coach carefully analyzed the game.

15. He cheerfully complimented Bashon, the pitcher.

16. Shyly, Bashon hung his head.

17. Kelsey gently patted Bashon on the back.

18. David laughingly called Bashon "Mr. Modest."

19. The coach then ended the meeting.

20. Gleefully, Brandon raced to his older brother.

C. **Write each sentence. Add an adverb in each blank.**

21. Brandon _____ threw his arms around David's legs.

22. "Little pal!" David _____ said as he patted Brandon.

23. "Let's go out for a snack," their mom _____ suggested.

24. "Race you to the car," Brandon _____ challenged.

25. David and Brandon _____ began their race.

Adverbs That Modify Adjectives and Adverbs

A. Write the word that is modified by each underlined adverb.

1. The park manager mailed us a <u>completely</u> revised brochure.

2. The summer activities were <u>very</u> clearly described.

3. By reading it <u>incredibly</u> carefully, I saw something interesting.

4. I was <u>extremely</u> excited about a new class, called AerobiKids.

5. The class was <u>quite</u> wisely offered on Saturday mornings.

6. The class was open <u>only</u> to kids aged ten to twelve.

7. An <u>extremely</u> enthusiastic instructor was to teach it.

8. The fee to enroll in the class was <u>rather</u> low.

9. My mom was <u>remarkably</u> encouraging about my need to enroll in the new class.

10. I was <u>amazingly</u> eager for the class to start!

B. Write the adverb and the word it modifies in each sentence.

11. I quite cheerfully jumped out of bed.

12. It was my very first day at AerobiKids.

13. My older sister quite kindly gave me a ride.

14. The room was very nearly packed with kids.

15. Our instructor was thoroughly perky.

16. She wore a really unusual microphone.

17. It was strapped remarkably tightly around her jaw.

18. It left her arms completely free to move.

19. She said our arms would be in almost constant motion.

20. Some of the exercises were too difficult for me.

C. Write each sentence. Underline each adverb that modifies an adjective or another adverb. Write *ADJ* above each modified adjective. Write *ADV* above each modified adverb.

21. The gymnastics teacher rather quickly taught us a new routine.

22. I was very confident in her gymnastic abilities.

23. I was somewhat nervous on my first attempt.

24. I know that my fitness will almost certainly improve.

25. After all the exercise, my legs are slightly sore today.

Comparing with Adverbs

A. **Write the correct comparative and superlative form of each adverb.**

1. fast
2. soon
3. late
4. happily
5. well

6. smoothly
7. excitedly
8. sweetly
9. brightly
10. badly

B. **Write each sentence. Use the correct form of the adverb.**

11. Jason types (more skillfully, most skillfully) than Keith.

12. He updates our homepage the (faster, fastest) of all.

13. Kevin adds information (more quickly, most quickly) than Tory.

14. The teacher held a contest to see who could create the (more beautifully, most beautifully) decorated Web page.

15. The (more carefully, most carefully) designed Web page of all was done by Kim.

16. Hers was (more creatively, most creatively) done than Tory's.

17. The (more humorously, most humorously) drawn cartoon of all appeared on Diego's Web page.

18. Carlo painted well, but Adriana painted (better, best).

19. Adriana added details (more frequently, most frequently) than her classmates.

20. The (most amazingly, more amazingly) animated page was Tina's.

C. **Write each sentence by using the correct form of the adverb in parentheses.**

21. Jason works the _____ of all on the computer. (proficiently)

22. The three friends worked _____ on Friday than they had on Tuesday. (cooperatively)

23. They worked _____ at school than at home. (eagerly)

24. The sixth grade planned its project _____ than the seventh grade. (carefully)

25. Making a Web page is one of the _____ satisfying experiences. (completely)

Negatives

A. **Write the word that correctly completes each sentence.**

1. Haven't you (ever, never) heard of the dog known as a Lhasa Apso?

2. Haven't you ever read (any, no) books about dogs?

3. We didn't have (any, no) trouble finding dog books.

4. I (could, couldn't) hardly believe how much information I found.

5. We didn't have (a, no) dog before we got Nikki.

6. We never had a cat, (either, neither).

7. We knew (anyone, no one) who had a Lhasa Apso.

8. My mother didn't know of (any, no) breeders to contact.

9. We weren't able to find (anything, nothing) about breeders in the newspaper.

10. We didn't learn (anything, nothing) from the Internet except that Lhasa Apsos were from Tibet.

B. **Write each sentence using the correct word.**

11. You (can, can't) hardly believe how entertaining Lhasas are!

12. I didn't think (any, no) dog would be as loyal this one.

13. Nikki hasn't (ever, never) forgotten to greet me.

14. I (can, can't) hardly wait to get home to see her.

15. My dog isn't (anything, nothing) like I imagined.

16. She doesn't (never, ever) bark unless she's lonely.

17. I try to (ever, never) leave her by herself.

18. We didn't know (nothing, anything) about dogs.

19. I couldn't think of (anyone, no one) who had a Lhasa.

20. I (could, couldn't) hardly have expected such a great pet.

C. **Rewrite each sentence. Correct the double negative.**

21. I can't hardly believe a small dog has such a loud bark!

22. Nikki doesn't never bark unless she's alarmed.

23. My dog hardly never leaves her post at the front window.

24. She doesn't bark or whine at no one.

25. Nikki won't ever bark at nobody.

Extra Practice

Colons and Hyphens

A. Write each sentence or phrase correctly by adding a colon or hyphen.

1. Dear Ms. Baker

2. Dear Professor Rosenthal

3. My sister in law, Cathy, is a gymnast.

4. The gymnast performs a state of the art routine.

5. Cathy practiced her routine twenty five times.

6. Jesse, Eduardo, and I are going to the last gym nastics meet.

7. Jesse called me about 800 last night to make plans.

8. Eduardo is a first rate driver.

9. He drives an older, blue green car.

10. His father is an attorney at law.

B. Write each sentence. Add a colon or a hyphen.

11. The gymnastics meet will begin at 1200.

12. Eduardo and I will pick up Jesse at 1115.

13. Eduardo would like to arrive at the meet by 1145.

14. We pulled up at Jesse's two story house.

15. Jesse's green eyed cat watched us from the window.

16. Since Eduardo has a two door car, I jumped out.

17. Eduardo is twenty one years old.

18. Jesse brought three things a wallet, a cap, and a sweater.

19. Eduardo played his brand new CD for us.

20. We arrived at the meet promptly at 1135.

C. Rewrite the letter. Add colons and hyphens where needed.

21–25. Dear Mrs. Ross

We went to a gymnastics meet at 1200 today. We sat on the left hand side of the gym, where my freckle faced friend, Cathy, was to perform her world-class floor routine. We saw the follow ing events parallel bars, pommel horse, rings, and uneven bars.

Sincerely,

Tony

Prepositions

A. **Write the preposition in each sentence.**

1. We're studying the United States Constitution in school.

2. The Constitution plays an important role in our lives.

3. It promises specific rights to all United States citizens.

4. It outlines the basic laws and principles of our nation.

5. The United States Constitution was written in 1787.

6. The Constitution replaced the Articles of Confederation.

7. After the Revolution, it was feared that the country would not last.

8. The country was then just a confederation of thirteen states.

9. Many important leaders gathered for a meeting.

10. Among themselves, they discussed the country's problems.

B. **Write the sentences. Circle the prepositions.**

11. The finest representatives from each state came to the meeting.

12. The meeting was held in the city of Philadelphia.

13. The meeting was known as the Constitutional Convention.

14. It lasted from May through September.

15. George Washington came to the meeting from Virginia.

16. Benjamin Franklin was a famous citizen of Philadelphia.

17. Thomas Jefferson was not among those who gathered for the meeting.

18. Jefferson was traveling in Europe during the meeting.

19. George Washington was elected president at the Convention.

20. The Convention was held in Independence Hall.

C. **Write each sentence. Fill in the blank with a preposition that makes sense.**

21. The Constitution had to be ratified _____ nine states.

22. _____ those who opposed the Constitution was Patrick Henry.

23. The first ten amendments were added _____ 1791.

24. The first ten amendments are known _____ the Bill of Rights.

25. Through the years, the Constitution has protected the rights _____ all people.

Extra Practice

Prepositional Phrases

A. **Write each sentence. Underline the adjective phrase. Circle the noun or pronoun it modifies.**

1. Ben read the myth on page 112.
2. The myth concerned the daughter of a king.
3. The king ruled the people of Jasmer.
4. His daughter was a woman of great speed.
5. She was fast and had a love of racing.
6. The daughter made a promise to her father.
7. She would marry a man with great running abilities.
8. Many with high hopes raced the princess.
9. The girl with incredible speed won every race.
10. One day the princess met a runner of great ability.

B. **Write the word or words that each underlined adverb phrase modifies. Label the word or words _verb_, _adjective_, or _adverb_.**

11. Today's orchestra rehearsal will be fun for Niko.
12. With great anticipation, he thinks about the rehearsal.
13. The orchestra consists of twelve students.
14. They rehearse after school.
15. The orchestra practices in the band room.
16. Niko arrives a bit early for the rehearsal.
17. Niko places music stands around the room.
18. Niko adds sheet music to the stands.
19. The other orchestra members come into the room.
20. The group plays beautiful music for their teacher.

C. **Write each sentence. Add a prepositional phrase in each blank.**

21. The runner was the prince _____.
22. He was the mightiest runner _____.
23. The race _____ ended in a tie.
24. He tilted his head slightly _____.
25. The race lasted _____.

Punctuation in Prepositional Phrases and Interjections

A. Write the sentences. Add a comma or an exclamation point to each sentence.

1. For our last field trip we visited the Art Institute.

2. Before the trip our art teacher discussed what we would see.

3. My goodness We saw some beautiful photographs.

4. With an overhead projector Ms. Lester shared her slides.

5. To prepare for our visit to the museum we studied works of art.

6. Boy I certainly learned a lot before we even went to the museum.

7. Of all the artists I liked Vincent van Gogh the best.

8. Wow He created many incredible self-portraits.

9. In some of the portraits he looks quite sad.

10. In his eyes you can see a sad expression.

B. Write each sentence. Add a comma or exclamation mark to set off a prepositional phrase or an interjection.

11. Gosh This is my favorite piece by Vincent van Gogh.

12. Wow The painting *First Steps* always fascinates me.

13. With its pale colors this painting has a soothing quality.

14. On the left side a crouching man seems to be waiting.

15. With outstretched arms he waits for a child.

16. Look His spade is on the ground next to him.

17. Behind the child a woman is holding the toddler by the arms.

18. My goodness The woman is helping the child take his first steps.

19. With outstretched arms and an upright head he looks determined.

20. Whoa I think the baby's first steps will be a success.

C. Write the sentences correctly.

21. Hey Who's your favorite artist?

22. Other than Vincent van Gogh whom do you like?

23. From my point of view van Gogh was the best artist of his time.

24. Wow I just love to study van Gogh's lovely oil creations.

25. Oh I also like the art of Paul Gauguin.

Build Skills

Maps and Atlases

DEFINITIONS AND FEATURES

- A map is a drawing or a diagram of a place.
- Maps show the names and locations of cities, rivers, mountains, and other important features of a geographical area.
- You can use the scale of miles, legend, and compass rose to locate features and to determine distances and directions.
- An atlas is a reference book that contains maps and information about geographical regions.
- Use the index of an atlas to find the map you need.

This map of Canada is from an atlas, a book of maps.

The key shows what the symbols on the map mean.

The scale of miles helps you find the distances between places on the map.

The compass rose indicates directions on the map.

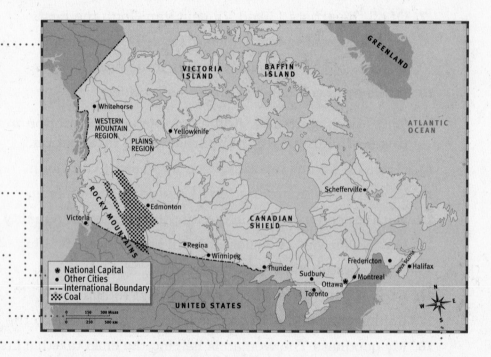

Practice Use the map to answer the following questions.

1. Which ocean is on Canada's east coast?

2. What is the national capital of Canada? How do you know?

3. In which region is Whitehorse?

4. What mineral is found in the Rocky Mountains?

5. In miles, what is the distance from Regina to Winnipeg?

Graphs

Build Skills

DEFINITIONS AND FEATURES

- A graph is a drawing that shows how kinds of information are related. There are several kinds of graphs.
- A graph has a title and labels to help you understand the information.
- There are several types of graphs. Circle graphs show percentages of a larger number. Line graphs use lines to show how numbers are related.

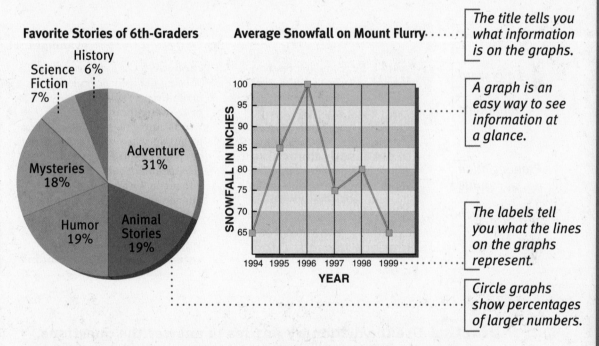

Favorite Stories of 6th-Graders

History 6%
Science Fiction 7%
Adventure 31%
Mysteries 18%
Humor 19%
Animal Stories 19%

Average Snowfall on Mount Flurry

The title tells you what information is on the graphs.

A graph is an easy way to see information at a glance.

The labels tell you what the lines on the graphs represent.

Circle graphs show percentages of larger numbers.

Practice Use the graphs to answer the following questions.

1. Which types of stories were the most popular?
2. Which types of stories were the least popular?
3. What percentage of 6th-graders liked animal stories?
4. In what year did the most snow fall on Mount Flurry?
5. How many more inches of snow fell during 1995 than during 1999?

Build Skills

Dictionary

DEFINITIONS AND FEATURES

- A **dictionary** gives the **meanings** and **pronunciations** of words.
- The words in dark type are called **entry words**. They are listed **alphabetically**.
- The two **guide words** at the top of the page show the first and last entry word on the page.
- The **pronunciation key** in the dictionary explains what the pronunciation symbols mean.

Guide words

Entry word

Definitions

Pronunciation guide

Part of speech

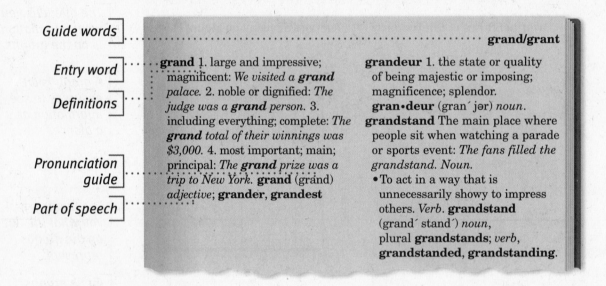

grand/grant

grand 1. large and impressive; magnificent: *We visited a **grand** palace.* 2. noble or dignified: *The judge was a **grand** person.* 3. including everything; complete: *The **grand** total of their winnings was $3,000.* 4. most important; main; principal: *The **grand** prize was a trip to New York.* **grand** (gránd) *adjective*; **grander**, **grandest**

grandeur 1. the state or quality of being majestic or imposing; magnificence; splendor. **gran•deur** (gran´ jər) *noun*. **grandstand** The main place where people sit when watching a parade or sports event: *The fans filled the grandstand. Noun.*
- To act in a way that is unnecessarily showy to impress others. *Verb.* **grandstand** (grand´ stand´) *noun*, plural **grandstands**; *verb*, **grandstanded**, **grandstanding**.

Practice Use the dictionary entries to answer the questions.

1. Which word would appear before this page: *granule, grammar,* or *grape*?

2. Which meaning of *grand* is used in this sentence? *A grand total of ten people attended my birthday party.*

3. How many syllables does *grandeur* have? How do you know?

4. What part of speech is *grandeur*?

5. How can you tell that *grandstand* can be used as a verb?

Bibliography

DEFINITIONS AND FEATURES

- The bibliography is a list of all the sources you have used to research and write a report. It may include books, articles, or other media resources.
- The bibliography tells your readers where you found your information and provides them with a guide to find out more.
- Entries are normally listed alphabetically by author. When no author is given, list an entry by its title.
- The bibliography gives the names of the authors, the title of the book or article, the publisher, the place of publication, and the copyright date of the material.

Newspaper article ········

Book ········

Magazine article ········

BIBLIOGRAPHY

Barna, Luisa. "Lacrosse Team Discovers Origins." *Jasper Daily Gazette*, April 15, 1999, p. 32.

Barrow, Amy and Lev Wolski. *Sports and Cultures Around the World*. Putney, VT: Diverse Traditions, 1996.

Native American Sports. New York: Painted Feather Press, 1987.

Player, Stanley. "Kick and Score: Kiowa Stick Games." *Native American Quarterly*, Fall 1989, pp. 120–136.

Running Bear, Henry. *Traditional Indian Games*. Chicago: Blue Hill Group, 2000.

Practice Use the sample bibliography to answer the following questions.

1. Which company published *Traditional Indian Games*?

2. When was Luisa Barna's article published?

3. In which source did the author find information about the Kiowa tribe?

4. Who co-wrote *Sports and Cultures Around the World*?

5. Which source is the oldest? When was it published?

Build Skills

On-Line Searches

DEFINITIONS AND FEATURES

- You can use a search engine to find a Web site about a specific topic. Type in keywords, then press RETURN or click on the SEARCH button.
- If your search turns up too many Web sites, refine your search by typing in more specific words. You can also place the exact words of your subject in quotation marks.
- You can search on-line newspapers to find news articles about particular topics or articles that were published on a certain date.
- Many on-line encyclopedias have search engines you can use to find articles about certain topics.

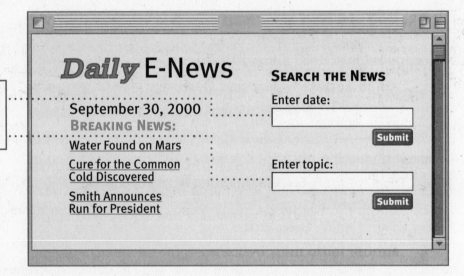

Enter a topic or a date to search for newspaper articles.

Daily E-News

September 30, 2000
BREAKING NEWS:

Water Found on Mars

Cure for the Common Cold Discovered

Smith Announces Run for President

SEARCH THE NEWS

Enter date:

[Submit]

Enter topic:

[Submit]

Practice Read each of the topics. Write *search engine, on-line newspaper*, or *on-line encyclopedia* to name the best way to search the Internet for information on that topic.

1. Yellowstone National Park
2. the scores from baseball games played yesterday
3. general information about the circulatory system
4. what happened when Mount St. Helens erupted
5. addresses of museums in your city

Reference Resources

DEFINITIONS AND FEATURES

- When you are conducting research, remember to use two or more sources to find and verify information.
- Match the resources you use to the purpose of your research. An encyclopedia, for example, gives a brief overview of a topic, while a nonfiction book may provide more in-depth information.
- Decide how current your information needs to be. Look at copyright dates for the most up-to-date information.
- Besides books, use other sources of information, such as interviews with experts, web sites, and videotapes.

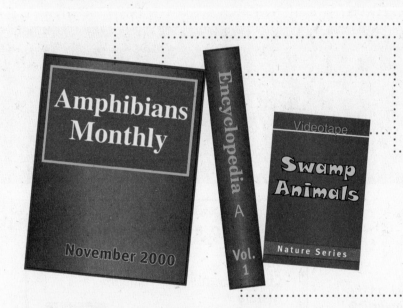

A magazine gives up-to-date information about topics.

Use two or more resources to support your research.

Use an encyclopedia to find general information about a subject.

Practice Read the following topics. Write *nonfiction book, magazine, newspaper, encyclopedia, videotape, interview,* or *atlas* to name the best source of information about that topic.

1. information about Mount Everest

2. a local zoologist's tips on feeding birds that visit your yard

3. an article about regional lakes that are good for fishing

4. the topic of the President's latest speech

5. large amounts of in-depth information about track-and-field events

Build Skills

Build Skills

Encyclopedia

DEFINITIONS AND FEATURES

- An encyclopedia is either print or electronic, and includes information about people, places, things, and events.
- Encyclopedia articles are about specific topics. In print versions, they are in books called volumes. Encyclopedia volumes are arranged in alphabetical order.
- Encyclopedia articles are arranged in alphabetical order by keywords. Each keyword is the main topic of an article. Search for a person by last name, unless they have only one name.

In this volume, you will find topics that begin with W, X, Y, and Z.

When you click on the "Submit" button, an article about Vikings will appear.

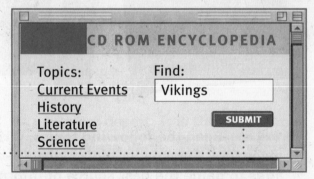

Practice Write the keyword that you would use to find information about each subject. Then write the number of the volume in which you would find the entry.

1. the names of Michelangelo's most famous works of art

2. the history of the South American country Bolivia

3. how the human eye works

4. the principal exports of Peru

5. Indira Gandhi's place in world history

Library Media Center

DEFINITIONS AND FEATURES

- A library or a media center includes a variety of materials and resources arranged in different sections.
- The card catalog is an alphabetical listing of the materials in the library. It may be in drawers or on a computerized database.
- The Dewey Decimal classification system sorts materials into ten main subject classes. The call numbers help you locate books. Fiction is arranged alphabetically.
- A periodical is a magazine or journal. The Readers' Guide to Periodical Literature lists every periodical in the library.
- The reference section includes books for research such as encyclopedias, atlases, dictionaries, and almanacs.

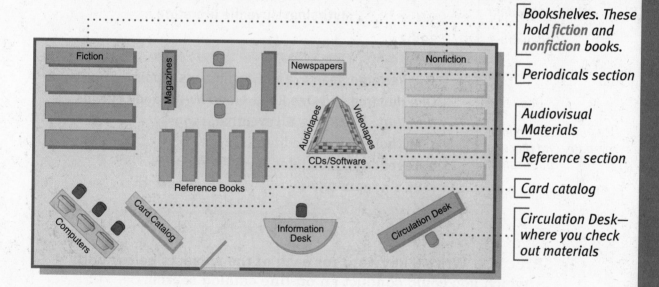

Practice Look at the floor plan above. Write where you would find each of the following items in the library.

1. a science CD-ROM

2. a collection of short stories

3. the current issue of *Time* magazine

4. a videotape about grizzly bears

5. a thesaurus

Study Skills

Build Skills

Card Catalog

DEFINITIONS AND FEATURES

- The card catalog is an alphabetical list of the materials that you can find in a particular library. Most libraries have electronic card catalogs.
- The entries are arranged by title, by author, and by subject. You can search for materials using only subject words if you do not know the titles or authors of books about certain topics.
- The computerized entries tell you where to find the materials. The call numbers tell you locations on the bookshelves.
- Some libraries have printed card catalogs. Entries are filed in drawers. The drawers are arranged alphabetically.

Subject heading	**Mythology-Juvenile literature**
Call number	**398.2**
Authors' names	**Verniero, Joan C. and Fitzsimmons, Robin**
Book title	**One Hundred and One Read-Aloud Myths and Legends**
Publisher's name, date, and place of publication	**New York: Black Dog & Leventhal, 1999**
	1. Mythology-Juvenile literature
	2. Legends and folktales-Juvenile literature
Subject headings	**ISBN 1-579912-057-1**

Practice Write a keyword for each of the subjects below with which you could conduct an on-line catalog search.

1. the San people of Australia

2. the U.S. Civil War battle of Antietam

3. treasures found in King Tutankhamen's tomb in Egypt

4. Julius Caesar, Roman Emperor

5. Alexander Graham Bell's invention of the telephone

240

Note-Taking

DEFINITIONS AND FEATURES

- Write questions you want to answer about the topic. Think of sources that will help you answer your questions.
- You can take notes from written material or a speaker for a research report. Use note cards.
- Put quotation marks around the author's exact words. Summarize the author's points in your own words when possible.
- Use your note cards to create an outline. Organize ideas by main topics and subtopics.
- Use your outline as a guide as you write your report.

Robert Hendrickson, Encyclopedia of Word and Phrase Origins ····· Source of notes
(New York: Facts on File, Inc., 1997), p. 236.

Wyoming—
Called the Equality State: Territorial Legislature was the first ····· Notes in note-
                  to grant women the vote in 1863. taker's words
                  Called Suffrage State for rather than
                  same reason. author's

Practice **Answer the following questions.**

1. After you identify a topic, what should you do to guide your research?

2. Why would you want to use more than one source?

3. From what source are these notes taken?

4. What question does the researcher want answered?

5. Why is it important to take notes?

Build Skills

Build Skills

Interviews

DEFINITIONS AND FEATURES

- An interview is a conversation between two or more people that can be an important part of research.
- The interviewer is the person who asks the questions.
- The subject of the interview is the person being questioned.
- Prepare simple and direct interview questions before you begin. Some questions will occur to you during the interview.
- Use notecards to record questions and answers during the interview. Use a tape recorder, if possible.

Name of subject ···· Interview with Dr. Moses   date: January 23, 2001

Date and time of the interview. ···· time: 3:45 PM

Purpose of the interview ···· Purpose: To find out as much as I can about becoming a veterinarian

Always have plenty of questions prepared in advance. ···· Questions: 1. What is a veterinarian?

2. What training is needed?

Leave space between your questions for taking notes during the interview. ···· 3. What is a typical day like for you?

4. What do you like most about your profession?

Practice Write two questions you would ask each of these people in an interview.

1. your student council president

2. the mayor of your town or city

3. the school nurse

4. the President of the United States

5. a local police officer

Periodicals

DEFINITIONS AND FEATURES

- A **periodical** is a newspaper, magazine, or journal published at regular intervals, such as weekly, monthly, or quarterly. Periodicals provide **current information** about topics.
- The **Readers' Guide to Periodical Literature** is a set of books or an electronic database that alphabetically lists, by topic or author, articles published in periodicals. It identifies the magazine, issue, and page where an article can be found.
- You can use a **newspaper index** to find newspaper articles about topics or by particular authors.
- **Media resources** are nonprint resources that you can use to find information, such as CD-ROMs, videotapes, and audiotapes.

Sample *Readers' Guide* Page

Egyptian art
"Treasures from the Age of Pyramids." Bennett Schiff *Smithsonian*
30:108–19 S '99
See also: **Pyramid art**

Subject entry
Article title
Periodical name
Author's name
Year of publication
"See also" gives cross-referencing information
Page number(s)
Volume number

Practice After each number in parentheses is a different part of a page from the *Readers' Guide.* Number your paper from 1 to 10. Identify the different parts of these *Readers' Guide* entries.

(1) Tornadoes

(2) "Terrible Twisters." **(3)** Monique Cline **(4)** *Time*

(5) 77:100-01 Ap '99

"Tornado Hits Little Rock."

(6) Dierdre Scotti *Newsweek* **(7)** 83: **(8)** 82–91

(9) Je '99 **(10)** *See also* **Storms**

Build Skills

RULE 1

Time-Order Words

- A time-order word explains the order in which events take place or tells when events occur.
- Sometimes a phrase can show time order in a piece of writing.

Time-Order Words and Phrases

first	as soon as	now
second	today	meanwhile
third	yesterday	before
next	tomorrow	after
last	finally	long ago

RULE 2

How Language Changes

- Language changes to meet the needs of people—new discoveries and new ideas demand new vocabulary.
- New words can be formed in different ways.

Type of Word	Definition	Examples
Compound Word	two or more short words combined	air + port = airport control + tower = control tower
Clipped Word	shortened form of other word	airplane⟶plane champion⟶champ
Blended Word	two words combined with some letters deleted	smoke + fog = smog breakfast + lunch = brunch
Borrowed Word	word from language other than English	ranch (Spanish) moccasins (Algonquin)

244

RULE 3 — Prefixes and Suffixes

- A prefix is a word part added to the beginning of a base word.
- A suffix is a word part added to the end of a base word.
- Adding a prefix or suffix changes the meaning of the base word to which it is added.

Prefix	Meaning	Suffix	Meaning
re-	again, back	-er, -or	one who, that which
un-, dis-, non-	not, the opposite of	-ful	full of
mis-	wrongly, badly	-able, -ible	capable of, fit for
pre-	before	-ness	state or quality of
bi-	having two of; twice	-less	without, not having
im-, in-	not, without, in, into	-ist	one who works at
post-	after	-ment	the act, state, quality, or result of
ex-	previous	-ward	moving or tending towards

RULE 4 — Synonyms and Antonyms

- Synonyms are words that have the same or almost the same meanings.
- Antonyms are words that have opposite meanings.
- A word may have more than one synonym or antonym.

Word	Synonym	Antonym
towering	tall	short
ancient	old	modern
empty	vacant	full
bright	sparkling	dull
magnificent	splendid	shabby
roomy	spacious	cramped

Build Skills

RULE 5

Roots

- **Roots** are word parts to which suffixes, prefixes, and other word parts can be added.
- You can figure out the **meaning** of a word by **figuring out** the meanings of the root, prefix, and suffix.

Roots	Meaning	Example
aud	"to hear"	auditorium, audience, audible
dict	"to tell"	dictionary, dictate, diction, predict
loc	"place"	local, relocate, location
ped	"foot"	pedometer, pedestrian, pedal
port	"carry"	support, report, portable, import, export
pose	"to put"	compose, position, repose
spect	"to look"	inspect, inspector, spectator
scribe, script	"to write"	describe, scribble, manuscript, description

RULE 6

Build Skills

Word Choice

- Good word choice depends on knowing the differences between words.
- Choose the word that most precisely expresses the meaning you intend.
- You might need to choose between synonyms, words that have the same or almost the same meaning.
- Some synonyms have different connotations. A connotation is the shade of meaning, or the feeling or overtone, created by a word.
- A connotation may be positive (inexpensive) or negative (cheap).

Positive Connotation	Negative Connotation
lively	rowdy
thrifty	stingy
slender	bony
aroma	stench
curious	nosy
relax	loaf
antique	old
clever	tricky
perform	show off
crowd	mob

Build Skills

Problem Words

- The English language includes some confusing words that are often misused. The charts show how these words are used properly.

Words	Correct Usage
accept	*Accept* means "to receive" or "to agree to." It is a verb. *I accept your apology.*
except	*Except* means "other than." It is usually a preposition. *I like all vegetables except Brussels sprouts.*
affect	*Affect* is a verb that means "to influence." *Your study habits will affect your grades.*
effect	*Effect* is a noun. It means "result or outcome." *The icy bridges are an effect of freezing temperatures.*
all ready	*All ready* means "all prepared." *The students were all ready to get on the bus.*
already	*Already* is an adverb that means "previously." *The teachers had already left.*
beside	*Beside* means "on the side of." *Our car is beside the curb.*
besides	*Besides* means "in addition to." *At the party, we will offer foods besides chicken.*
can	*Can* tells about an ability. *Juan can run faster than me.*
may	*May* expresses permission. *You may go outside when you finish your homework.*
fewer	*Fewer* is used for things that can be counted. *Sara has fewer pencils than Janice.*
less	*Less* is used for things or ideas that cannot be counted. *I am less athletic than Rene is.*
good	Good is an adjective that describes something positive. *Brian's painting was very good.*
well	*Well* is usually an adverb. It gives more information about the verb by telling "how." *My little sister has learned to read quite well.*

Build Skills

Problem Words

Words	Correct Usage
lay	*Lay* means "to put something down." Lay *the towels on the table.*
lie	*Lie* means "to recline or rest." Lie *on the blanket and look up at the stars.*
many	*Many* is used with nouns that can be counted. *Alex planned* many *games for the party guests.*
much	*Much* is used with nouns that cannot be counted. *There was* much *laughter during the party.*
precede	*Precede* means "to come or go before someone or something." *The sixth graders will* precede *the fifth graders in the parade.*
proceed	*Proceed* means "to go on, usually without interruption." *You may now* proceed *with the test.*
principal	*Principal* refers to the "head officer of a school." *Mr. Wright is our school* principal.
principle	A *principle* is "a basic truth or law by which a person lives." *Our country is based on a* principle *of individual rights.*
raise	*Raise* means "to cause to move upward." *The boys want to* raise *the height of the basketball goal.*
rise	*Rise* means "to move upward." *Let's blow bubbles and watch them* rise.
set	*Set* means "to put something down or in a certain place." *I* set *my drink on the table.*
sit	*Sit* means "to be seated." *Please* sit *down so we can start class.*

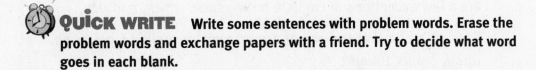

QUICK WRITE   Write some sentences with problem words. Erase the problem words and exchange papers with a friend. Try to decide what word goes in each blank.

Build Skills

RULES

▶ **Silent e** When words *end in silent e*, drop the *e* when adding an ending that begins with a vowel. *(pursue + ed = pursued)* When adding an ending that begins with a consonant, keep the silent *e* *(agile + ly = agilely)*.

▶ **Spelling with y** When a base word *ends with a consonant followed by y*, change the *y* to *i* when adding any ending except endings that begin with *i*. *(cry + es = cries; cry + ing = crying)* When a base word *ends with a vowel followed by y*, do not change the *y* when adding endings. *(monkey + s = monkeys)*

▶ **Vowel and Final Consonant** When a one-syllable word *ends in one vowel followed by one consonant*, double the consonant before adding an ending that begins with a vowel. *(run + ing = running)*

▶ **The letter q** is always followed by *u*. *(quilt, equip)*

▶ No English word ends in *j*, *q*, or *v*.

▶ **Plural and Verb Tense** Add *-s* to most words to form plurals or to change the tense of verbs. Add *-es* to words ending in *x*, *z*, *s*, *sh*, or *ch*. *(cup + s = cups; box + es = boxes; watch + es = watches)*

▶ **Plural: f and fe** To make plurals of words that end with one *f* or *fe*, you often need to change the *f* or *fe* to *v* and add *-es*. *(life + es = lives)*

▶ **ie and ei Words** When choosing *ei* or *ie*, remember that *i* comes before *e* except after *c* or when it sounds like /ā/ as in n**ei**ghbor or w**ei**gh.

▶ **The /s/ Sound** When the /s/ *sound* is spelled *c*, *c* is always followed by *e*, *i*, or *y*. *(peace, circular, fancy)*

▶ **When /j/ is Spelled g** *g* is always followed by *e*, *i*, or *y*. *(generous, engine, energy)*

▶ **The /ch/ Sound** If the /ch/ sound immediately follows a short vowel in a one-syllable word, it is spelled *tch*. *(latch, clutch)* There are a few exceptions in English: *much*, *such*, *which*, and *rich*.

▶ **The /f/ sound** at the end of a word may be spelled *f*, *ph*, or *gh*. *(brief, graph, trough)*

RULES

Use these strategies to help you become a better speller.

▶ **Homophones** Learn common homophones and make sure you have used the correct homophone in your writing. *(They're having fun with their toys. I see them over there.)*

▶ **Rhyming Words** Think of a word you know that has the same spelling pattern as the word you want to spell, such as a rhyming word. *(jiggle, wiggle, giggle)*

▶ **Use words that you know** how to spell to help you spell new words. *(flower + clock = flock)*

▶ **Make up clues** to help you remember the spelling. *(ache = a cat has ears; u play guitar; a piece of pie; our gourd)*

▶ **Related Words** Think of a related word to help you spell a word with a silent letter or a hard-to-hear sound. *(sign-signal; relative-related)*

▶ **Syllables** Divide the word into syllables. *(in gred i ent)*

▶ **Prefixes and Suffixes** Learn to spell prefixes and suffixes you often use in writing.

▶ **Word Chunks** Look for word chunks or smaller words that help you remember the spelling of the word. *(hippopotamus = hippo pot am us)*

▶ **Change the way you say the word** to yourself to help with the spelling. *(knife = /k nīf/; beauty = /bē ū tē/)*

▶ **Visualizing** Think of the times you may have seen the word in reading, on signs, or in a textbook. Try to remember how it looked. Write the word in different ways. Which one looks correct? *(lern, larn, learn)*

▶ **Personal Word List** In a notebook, keep an alphabetical Personal Word List. List words you often have trouble spelling.

▶ **Dictionary** Become familiar with the dictionary and use it often. If you are working on a computer, use the spell-check program. Remember, though, that spell-checkers are not perfect. They cannot tell whether you have used a word correctly.

Build Skills

Easily Confused Words

- Some words are easily mistaken for one another because they are spelled similarly or they sound alike. These words have different definitions, so you need to be sure you use the correct one.

accent	all together	command	expand	recent
ascent	altogether	commend	expend	resent
accept	angel	continual	farther	respectively
except	angle	continuous	further	respectfully
access	any more	costume	later	suppose
excess	anymore	custom	latter	supposed
accuse	assistance	desert	lay	than
excuse	assistants	dessert	lie	then
advice	bazaar	device	loose	though
advise	bizarre	devise	lose	through
affect	breath	emigrant	moral	use
effect	breathe	immigrant	morale	used
alley	cease	envelop	pillar	vanish
ally	seize	envelope	pillow	varnish
all ready	clamber	era	quiet	your
already	clamor	error	quite	you're

Frequently Misspelled Words

- For many writers, some words are difficult to spell. You can use this list to check your spelling.

ache	entertainment	heard	planet	through
again	environment	height	probably	together
anything	especially	house	really	umbrella
argument	except	know	reason	upstairs
around	exciting	laboratory	receive	usually
awhile	favorite	library	religious	wear
beautiful	February	license	restaurant	were
because	field	lightning	schedule	where
beginning	finally	met	separate	whole
bored	foreign	meteor	sometimes	wouldn't
business	forty	myself	swimming	you're
clothes	friend	none	their	
college	guess	often	themselves	

Common Homophones

- Homophones are words that sound the same but have different spellings and meanings. *Whole* and *hole* are homophones.

air	capital	holy	peace	shone
heir	Capitol	wholly	piece	shown
aisle	choral	horse	peer	stake
I'll	coral	hoarse	pier	steak
isle				
allowed	cite	lie	pole	steal
aloud	sight	lye	poll	steel
	site			
band	coarse	mail	principal	throne
banned	course	male	principle	thrown
bass	colonel	missed	rain	vain
base	kernel	mist	reign	vane
			rein	vein
beat	council	no	rap	wade
beet	counsel	know	wrap	weighed
birth	die	pain	real	wail
berth	dye	pane	reel	whale
bite	foul	passed	ring	waist
byte	fowl	past	wring	waste
bolder	hoard	patience	shear	
boulder	horde	patients	sheer	

Word Study Steps

Be a better speller by following these steps.

1. Study each letter in the word.
2. Picture the word in your mind.
3. Write the word carefully.
4. Check the spelling of the word.

Build Skills

Correcting Sentence Fragments

Remember!

- A sentence is a group of words that expresses a complete thought.

- A sentence fragment does not express a complete thought.

Problem 1

A sentence fragment that does not have a subject

Sentence Fragment: *Visited my relatives in Texas.*

> *Who visited your relatives?*

Solution 1

You need to add a subject to the sentence fragment to make it a complete sentence.

Sentence: *My mom, dad, and I visited my relatives in Texas.*

Problem 2

A sentence fragment that does not have a predicate

Sentence Fragment: *The Spanish explorer Cabeza de Vaca.*

> *What about this Spanish explorer?*

Solution 2

You need to add a predicate to the sentence fragment to make it a complete sentence.

Sentence: *The Spanish explorer Cabeza de Vaca traveled across Texas.*

Troubleshooter

Problem 3

A sentence fragment that does not have a subject and a predicate

Sentence Fragment: *By the Spanish in 1821.*

Who or what is this about? What happened in 1821?

Solution 3

Add a subject and a predicate to the fragment to make it a complete sentence.

Sentence: *Texas was ruled by the Spanish in 1821.*

Practice **Rewrite the sentence fragments to make complete sentences.**

1. Visited a museum in Fort Worth, Texas.

2. Thought about the lives of the early settlers.

3. All of the students in my class.

4. Was an old Spanish fort in San Antonio.

5. Told us about the battle at the Alamo.

6. A huge map of the Rio Grande.

7. This enormous river.

8. Old pictures, documents, and exhibits.

9. Discussed what we had learned.

10. How people struggled for freedom.

Correcting Run-on Sentences

- A **sentence** is a group of words that expresses a complete thought.

- A **run-on sentence** contains two or more sentences that should stand alone.

Problem 1

Two sentences joined with no punctuation between them

Run-on Sentence: *Clara Barton was born in 1821 at that time few American women had careers.*

> Are there two complete thoughts in this sentence?

Solution 1

Separate the two complete thoughts into two sentences, and add the necessary capitalization and punctuation.

Sentences: *Clara Barton was born in 1821. At that time, few American women had careers.*

Problem 2

Two sentences joined only by a comma

Run-on Sentence: *Clara Barton became famous during the Civil War, the president recognized her service to the country.*

> Aren't these two different sentences?

Solution 2

Place a comma at the end of the first complete thought. Then add *and*, *but*, or *or* to connect the two thoughts.

Compound Sentence: *Clara Barton became famous during the Civil War, and the president recognized her service to the country.*

Problem 3

Three or more sentences joined with *and*, *but*, or *or*

Run-on Sentence: *Clara Barton cooked meals for the soldiers, and she even removed bullets from those who were wounded, and she comforted those who were dying.*

> Does this sentence include three separate thoughts connected by *and*?

Solution 3

Create more than one sentence by separating ideas and using correct end punctuation. Join two closely related ideas to form a compound sentence.

Separate Sentences: *Clara Barton cooked meals for the soldiers. She even removed bullets from those who were wounded, and she comforted those who were dying.*

Practice **Rewrite these run-on sentences correctly.**

1. Clara Barton started the Red Cross in 1882 she was its president for 23 years.

2. Clara Barton was 78 years old when a hurricane hit Texas, the Red Cross helped the survivors.

3. Clara Barton fought for those in need, she never stopped until she succeeded.

4. Barton was shy as a child she eventually overcame her shyness.

5. I enjoyed learning about Clara Barton, and my teacher gave us a lot of information, but I still wanted to know more.

Confusing Plurals and Possessives

Remember!

- A **plural noun** names more than one person, place, or thing and usually ends in *-s* or *-es*.

- A **possessive noun** shows who or what owns or has something.

- To form the possessive of most singular nouns, add an apostrophe and an *s* (*'s*).

- To form the possessive of a plural noun that ends in *-s*, add only an apostrophe (*'*). To form the possessive of a plural noun not ending in *-s*, add an apostrophe and an *s* (*'s*).

Problem 1

Using an apostrophe in a plural noun

Incorrect Plural Form: *Invention's improve the lives of many people.*

> Do the inventions have or own anything?

Solution 1

Remove the apostrophe. Do not use an apostrophe in a plural noun.

Correct Plural Form: *Inventions improve the lives of many people.*

Problem 2

Leaving out an apostrophe in a singular possessive noun

Incorrect Possessive Form: *Henry Fords invention was the Model-T Ford.*

> Does Henry Ford own or have something?

Solution 2

Correct a singular possessive noun by adding an apostrophe and an *s* (*'s*).

Correct Possessive Form: *Henry Ford's invention was the Model-T Ford.*

Troubleshooter

Problem 3

Putting the apostrophe in the wrong place in a plural possessive noun

Incorrect Form: *Many inventor's ideas have changed the world.*

Are we talking about one inventor or more than one inventor?

Solution 3

Correct a plural possessive that ends in *s* by adding an apostrophe after the *s* (*s'*). To correct a plural noun not ending in *-s*, add an apostrophe and an *s* (*'s*).

Correct Form: *Many inventors' ideas have changed the world.*

Practice Rewrite each sentence correctly. Use the correct plural or possessive form.

1. One inventor worked with scientist's to develop a quick-freezing method for preserving food.

2. This scientists invention changed the eating habits of people around the world.

3. Thanks to frozen foods, some childrens' diets have even improved.

4. Other scientist's ideas have also changed the way that we live.

5. It's hard to believe, but one inventors idea really can change the entire world.

Lack of Subject-Verb Agreement

Remember!

- A subject and verb must agree in a sentence.
- The subject and verb agree when both are singular or both are plural.

Problem 1

Using a singular verb with a plural subject or a plural verb with a singular subject

No Agreement: *Some explorers has sailed across uncharted seas.*

Is the subject singular or plural? What about the verb?

Solution 1

Change the singular verb to match the plural subject.

Subject-Verb Agreement: *Some explorers have sailed across uncharted seas.*

Problem 2

Using a singular verb with a compound subject joined by *and*

No Agreement: *Matthew Henson and Robert Peary was the first explorers to reach the North Pole.*

Is this subject plural or singular?

Solution 2

Change the singular verb to match the compound subject.

Subject-Verb Agreement: *Matthew Henson and Robert Peary were the first explorers to reach the North Pole.*

Troubleshooter

Problem 3

Using the wrong verb form with a compound subject joined by *or*, *either...or*, or *neither...nor*

No Agreement: *Neither the guide nor the explorers was well prepared.*

Should the verb agree with *guide* or *explorers*?

Solution 3

Use a verb that matches the subject closest to it.

Subject-Verb Agreement: *Neither the guide nor the explorers were well prepared.*

Practice **Rewrite each sentence to correct any errors in agreement.**

1. Arctic explorers needs rope, snow goggles, and a winter parka.

2. The blowing snow are sometimes blinding.

3. Ice-climbing boots is especially important.

4. Some people even wears more than one pair of socks.

5. Many explorers has found food by ice fishing.

6. Cod, halibut, and trout is found in the Arctic Ocean.

7. Neither the Arctic nor the deserts gets much rain.

8. During certain times of the year, the sun don't shine at all in the Arctic.

9. Either sled dogs or a snowmobile are useful when exploring the Arctic.

10. Someday my brother and I wants to explore the Arctic.

Incorrect Verb Forms

 **Remember!**

- An irregular verb is a verb that does not add *-d* or *-ed* to form the past tense and past participle.
- The best way to learn irregular verbs is to memorize them.

Problem 1

Forming irregular verbs incorrectly

Incorrect Verb Form: *Mr. Carson drived the children to the park.*

> Is *drived* the past tense of *drive*?

Solution 1

Irregular verbs do not follow a set pattern to form the past tense and the past participle. Memorize the forms, or look them up.

Correct Verb Form: *Mr. Carson drove the children to the park.*

Problem 2

Using the past-tense form instead of the past participle

Incorrect Verb Form: *I have saw some beautiful flowers in the park.*

> What form of *see* do you use with the word *have*?

Solution 2

When you use the helping verb *have*, use the past participle, not the past form.

Correct Verb Form: *I have seen some beautiful flowers in the park.*

Problem 3

Using the past participle incorrectly

Incorrect Verb Form: *I done my homework early.*

Is the word *done* used by itself or with the helping verb *have*?

Solution 3

Add the helping verb *has, have,* or *had* to the past participle of an irregular verb.

Correct Verb Form: *I have done my homework early.*

Practice **Rewrite the sentences using the correct verb forms.**

1. Last night, the moths flied around the light outside.
2. I taked my baby brother into the yard.
3. I knowed the moths would make him laugh.
4. After a while, I catched a moth for him.
5. He maked a funny face when I held it up.
6. I don't know what he thinked about it.
7. My brother had never saw the moths before.
8. By morning, they had goed away.
9. I have drew a picture of the moths for my brother.
10. He has took the picture to his room.

Incorrect Use of Adjectives That Compare

Remember!

- **Adjectives** can compare two or more people, things, or ideas.
- The **comparative** form of an adjective compares two nouns.
- The **superlative** form of an adjective compares more than two nouns.

Problem 1

Using *-er* or *-est* instead of *more* or *most*

> **Incorrect Form:** *I think birds are popularer than bugs.*

How do you make comparisons with an adjective such as popular?

Solution 1

Use *more* or *most* to form comparative and superlative adjectives with three or more syllables.

> **Correct Form:** *I think birds are more popular than bugs.*

Problem 2

Using *-er* or *-est* with *more* or *most*

> **Incorrect Form:** *This spider's web is more bigger than that one.*

How do you form a comparative adjective with the word big?

Solution 2

With shorter adjectives, add *-er* or *-est* to compare people, places or things. Never use *more* or *most* with *-er* or *-est*. Rewrite the sentence without *more*.

> **Correct Form:** *This spider's web is bigger than that one.*

Problem 3

Using the incorrect form when comparing with *good* or *bad*

Incorrect Form: *In the garden, some bugs are gooder than others.*

> What are the comparative and superlative forms of *good*?

Solution 3

The comparative forms of *good* and *bad* are *better* and *worse*. The superlative forms of *good* and *bad* are *best* and *worst*.

Correct Form: *In the garden, some bugs are better than others.*

Practice **Rewrite each sentence correctly.**

1. Mantises look frighteninger than other bugs.

2. However, mantises are the goodest bugs because they eat garden pests.

3. Mosquitoes are the annoyingest of all bugs.

4. Their bite is the baddest, too.

5. Fireants form the most largest anthills.

6. Ladybugs are the most pretty garden insects.

7. They're more smaller than other flying bugs.

8. Butterflies have delicater wings than moths.

9. Butterflies are the most colorfulest garden bug.

10. I think butterflies are the goodest bug to photograph.

Incorrect Use of Pronouns

Remember!

- The referent, or antecedent, of a pronoun is the word or group of words to which the pronoun refers.
- Use a subject pronoun when the pronoun is in the subject part of a sentence.
- Use an object pronoun when the pronoun is the object of a verb or preposition.

Problem 1

Using a pronoun that does not match its referent

Pronoun Does Not Match: *Sean wrote a report and gave them to the teacher.*

To which noun does them refer?

Solution 1

Replace the incorrect pronoun with a pronoun that clearly matches its referent.

Pronoun Match: *Sean wrote a report and gave it to the teacher.*

Problem 2

Using an object pronoun as the subject of a sentence

Incorrect Pronoun: *Him reported on rocks and minerals.*

Should the pronoun Him be used in subject or predicate parts?

Solution 2

Change the object pronoun to a subject pronoun because this pronoun is being used in the subject part of a sentence.

Correct Pronoun: *He reported on rocks and minerals.*

266

Problem 3

Using a subject pronoun in the predicate part

Incorrect Pronoun: *Lisa gave he a crystal to study.*

Is *he* a pronoun that should be used in the predicate part of a sentence?

Solution 3

Replace the subject pronoun with an object pronoun because this pronoun is the object of a verb.

Correct Pronoun: *Lisa gave him a crystal to study.*

Practice Rewrite each sentence correctly.

1. Amanda found a rock and gave her to the teacher.

2. The teacher showed the rock to the class and asked they to study it.

3. Her had been teaching the students all about gemstones.

4. Amanda's aunt gave she a jade necklace.

5. Amanda brought the necklace to school and showed them to her friends.

6. Jesse and me both looked for information about gems in our book.

7. Him found the articles and illustrations first.

8. Holding the pictures up, he showed it to Mrs. Walker.

9. The teacher then handed we a beautiful red gemstone.

10. Now us all look at rocks in exciting new ways.

Apostrophes

Remember!

- An **apostrophe** is used to show possession in nouns or to show letters that have been left out of a contraction.

- An **apostrophe** is not used in a possessive pronoun.

Problem 1

Leaving out apostrophes in contractions

Incorrect Form: *Im having fun solving these math problems!*

Is *I'm* a possessive pronoun or a contraction?

Solution 1

Contractions use apostrophes to show where the letters are left out. In this sentence, *Im* represents the words *I am*, so it needs an apostrophe.

Correct Form: *I'm having fun solving these math problems!*

Problem 2

Putting an apostrophe in a possessive pronoun

Incorrect Form: *Is the book on the table her's?*

Is there a possessive pronoun in this sentence?

Solution 2

Possessive pronouns do not contain apostrophes. Remove the apostrophe from the possessive pronoun.

Correct Form: *Is the book on the table hers?*

Problem 3

Confusing contractions and possessive pronouns

Incorrect Word: *You're book is on the table.*

> Does *You're* show possession or stand for *you are*?

Solution 3

Do not confuse the contractions *it's, you're,* and *they're* with the possessive pronouns *its, your,* and *their.* Use the possessive pronoun rather than the contraction in this sentence.

Correct Word: *Your book is on the table.*

Practice Rewrite each sentence correctly.

1. Matthew cant find his bicycle and his helmet.

2. Hes riding his bike to the park this afternoon.

3. Matthews friend Anita will come with him.

4. Shes already wearing her helmet.

5. Matthew doesnt see his helmet in the garage.

6. Next he looks for his bike, but its not in the garage.

7. "Your not going to find it there," his mom says.

8. "Their all in the basement now," Mom adds.

9. Anita says, "That's where we keep our's, too."

10. "Okay, Im ready," says Matthew. "Let's go!"

Incorrect Use of Adverbs

Remember!

- An **adverb** is a word that modifies a verb, an adjective, or another adverb.

- Adverbs tell *how*, *when*, *where*, or *to what extent*.

- Do not use two **negatives** in a sentence.

Problem 1

Confusing adjectives and adverbs

Incorrect Form: *Our principal treats everyone nice.*

> Is the word *nice* modifying the noun or the verb?

Solution 1

The verb, not the noun, is being modified. Replace the adjective with the correct adverb.

Correct Form: *Our principal treats everyone nicely.*

Problem 2

Using *good* instead of *well*

Incorrect Form: *I did good on the test.*

> Are we describing a noun or telling about the verb?

Solution 2

Good is always an adjective. *Well* is usually an adverb. Use *well* to modify the verb.

Correct Form: *I did well on the test.*

Problem 3

Using double negatives

Incorrect Form: *I didn't miss none of the problems.*

Solution 3

Do not use two negatives in one sentence. Remove one of the negative words, or replace it with a positive word.

Correct Form: *I didn't miss any of the problems.*

Are there two negatives in this sentence?

Practice   Rewrite each sentence correctly.

1. Our class walked quick to the nature preserve.

2. We were eagerly to see the animals.

3. Our guide was helpful and spoke clear.

4. He had a lot of information about unusually animals.

5. Everyone listened very attentive.

6. We quiet observed some animals in their habitats.

7. We enjoyed watching them in their naturally surroundings.

8. We didn't see no tigers, but we saw a lot of other animals.

9. We were allowed to speak gentle to some of the babies.

10. The guide said our class behaved good on the trip.

Commas

Remember!

- Use a **comma** to separate words that interrupt the flow of a sentence.

- Use a **comma** after a long introductory prepositional phrase.

- Use a **comma** after a mild interjection.

Problem 1

Using commas incorrectly

Incorrect Form: *This summer for instance we are going to California.*

Incorrect Form: *After our trip we are going to visit my grandparents.*

Incorrect Form: *Oh I can't wait to see them.*

> Do words interrupt the sentence flow? Is there a prepositional phrase or a mild interjection?

Solution 1

Use commas to set apart words that interrupt the flow of a sentence. Also use a comma after a long introductory prepositional phrase or a mild interjection.

Correct Form: *This summer, for instance, we are going to California.*

Correct Form: *After our trip, we are going to visit my grandparents.*

Correct Form: *Oh, I can't wait to see them!*

Practice Rewrite each sentence correctly.

1. Before we planned our trip we read a travel book.

2. California for instance is one of the most popular states to visit.

3. The journey of course will be long and tiring.

4. Before we arrive I will call my grandparents.

5. Gee California will be a fun place to visit.